CHANGING COURSE

A Spiritual Journey

GARY WATSON

outskirtspress

DENVER, COLORADO

Outskirts Press, Inc.
http://www.outskirtspress.com

ISBN: 978-1-4327-9373-9

Outskirts Press and the "OP" logo are trademarks belonging to Outskirts Press, Inc.

PRINTED IN THE UNITED STATES OF AMERICA

I would like to dedicate this book to Janice, (my wife of 28 years), and Laurel, (our daughter), who are the greatest loves in my life. It is also for my family who has shown love, support and understanding as I have ventured my path upon this earth. I would like, also, to gratefully acknowledge those people God has placed in my life that I have learned from and have stood beside me in my quest of spiritual living. Their time, patience, and unconditional love, have shown me how to place one foot in front of the other and actually held me up at times until I found my own path. It is for all those who choose a course of living spiritually. Perhaps most important of all, it is for those out there who still suffer and hunger for change. I ask God to use me as an instrument to deliver words of hope.

Table of Contents

Preface i

1: Free Will – Self Will 1

2: Prayer and Meditation 8

3: Gratitude 15

4: An inside job 23

5: Miracles 30

6: Faith 35

7: Love 42

8: Growth..51

9: Acceptance 58

10: Into the Mystic..63

11: Happiness 70

12: Humility..79

13: Unity and Service 86

14: Changing Course...95

Preface

My first book, "Dissolve into Evolving", was actually a primer to set the stage for the changes in our living to begin. It was also intended to be a foundation to build upon your own journey. I briefly discussed the "seven deadly sins" which are our character flaws, how they affect us and keep us in bondage of living in self- will instead of God's will. We came to understand they are poisons in our life that we must rid ourselves of if spiritual changes were to come about. We should also conclude that our efforts to live out of this bondage would be a life-long process, which requires daily maintenance. This we not only accomplish by prayer and meditation, but by taking responsibility and action as well. I had pointed out that "we cannot think our way into spiritual living" but rather "we live ourselves into spiritual thinking". It can be no other way.

It is my humble opinion we are here upon this earth to learn. Each one of us is a miracle, whether we realize this or not. We all have a purpose even though we may not clearly see it. Even so, it may take many years to discover what our purpose really is. Our lives are a gift and we are gifts to one another. It is also my belief that we can and do experience heaven and hell on this earth. I sincerely feel I have experienced both, and I would later realize my appreciation for both, because it was the most difficult of times that finally led to my personal defeat, true freedom, and awareness that God's intention for us is to live happy, joyous, and free lives. We are all going to witness pain and suffering at times and that is vital for spiritual growth; however, we are not destined to live in it constantly. We are not here to suffer. Grief from the loss of a loved one is certainly natural and we are all going to know those times but any discord in our lives is, or derives, from lies that we tell ourselves. How we do that and how we step out of it, is largely the purpose of this book. We find that what happens is that we go against the natural laws, which we only fool ourselves about and will certainly bring us pain and entrapment if left unchecked.

Many of us do, however, find ourselves living a life that is unhappy and miserable. We search for bandages we think will help us escape such as alcohol, drugs, risky sexual behavior and an array of other destructive behaviors we feel will help temporarily, but we fail to treat our underlying problems. These temporary fixes may work for a while but eventually, they work against us and multiply our misery. There is a solution! The depths some of us go to in order to find our answers vary. You do not have to go to a place many have known as "a rock bottom" to find the solution. It is always right there inside of us ready to work when sincerely called upon. The solution is God and He lives inside you and every human on this planet. All that is required of us is honesty and a little willingness for a great change to begin. Jesus had only one simple test for any situation. Does it work? As you reflect upon your life and find areas you are not happy with, you can apply this same test.

It is my hope that within this book you may find some words that will bring you closer to your gentle, all loving and forgiving Father, and that you pass along the truth you find to another in need. The blockage of self-will is all that stands in the way. The only thing you stand to lose is your misery, which is refundable at any time. It is also very important to understand that spirituality is the essence of simplicity. Most humans, including myself, seem to have a gift of attempting to complicate matters. This in itself clearly points out that we are trying to control our lives instead of letting God. Over the years, I have come to know this simple fact is a tool which helps to strengthen my faith. As everything else I have learned so far, it has come from trial and error. We are born into life with the gift of free will. Yet at any time we find we have created disaster, He is always there to guide us back to our path. God loves you enough to allow you to try to run your own life. It is within this system we come to realize that the old ways in which we have lived had to die that a new life of serenity could be born. Perhaps this is a part of the demonstration of the resurrection of Christ.

It is my opinion that faith and trust are qualities we have to earn. Likewise, all who possess faith also have courage. This is attained by taking chances with what we are not familiar. In the late nineteen eighties, I had lived my life to a point I found myself completely defeated. I honestly did not know if God existed or not. All I really knew was that the best I knew how to live my life had not worked. It was with blind faith and willingness from the depths of pain that I turned my life over to God. I had no idea of the power and source I was beginning to enter. After a period and a great deal of effort, I found myself living in a different dimension than I had ever known. What was at one time "blind faith" became dependence. It was at this time that I began a construction of my life, in that I was no longer running the show. Re-construction and re-habilitated are two words I seldom use because the truth of the matter is, many of us were never habilitated or properly instructed from the beginning. It is through the process of living life on life's terms that we become educated on what are truths and what is false. We do well to have gratitude for both. Just as the current of a river that over time polishes an ordinary rock into a smooth and beautiful stone, so it is with living spiritually. Celebrate both what you have and what you have not.

No one has our answers. Clergy, doctors, counselors and other mentors can guide us in a direction but ultimately we find that it is only by our own experiences and desire for change that the answers come to us. It is a simple matter of turning to God and they shall be revealed. It is our journey, our path, and our hunger for truth which shapes our destiny. All journeys begin by taking our first step and placing one foot in front of the other. There have been so many people in my life from whom I have gained a great deal of spiritual knowledge. However, there is no amount of knowledge which will substitute for the actual practice of principles in our daily living. This we do because we earnestly desire change. "Knock and it shall be opened". This simple promise from Jesus will never fail you. Nor will any of His teachings.

1 | Free Will - Self Will

Although these two concepts sound as though they are the same, there is a great difference. They can, and often do, become opposites. We are born with free will, which is perhaps our greatest gift. It is God given. The summation is our ability to make conscious, rightful choices. Referring back upon the simple test of Christ, "does it work" it clearly signifies that we have a choice in any given situation. He does not state that we cannot do something, nor did He say everything we do will have positive results. We are the ones who get to choose. Likewise, we are the ones who live with the decisions we make, which we also have the ability to change if we wish. I should also say here in the beginning, there are natural laws which do exist. We may act against them, but in reality we cannot break them, rather, we can only damage ourselves. This is so because we have a conscience. Before I go any further, there is another word and subject I will introduce which is sobriety. I find it almost impossible to distinguish the difference between free will and self- will without the awareness of this subject and its definitions.

When we hear the word sobriety, we immediately think of alcoholism or drug addiction. Its definition includes clearheadedness, sane rational thinking, abstinence, and another interesting word comes up which is gravity. The natural laws are our gravity. They allow us to remain grounded in principles upon which we live our lives. People become intoxicated in many different ways, including money, power, prestige, sex and a very wide assortment of other matters we allow to have far too much control over us. I am certainly not implying that our human gifts are not wonderful attributes to enjoy. All that God has blessed us with, we should be eternally grateful and enjoy. It is when we step outside the gravity that we allow ourselves to become plague ridden by character flaws and misfortune, which lead to discomfort and misery. What we many times fail to understand is these matters are practically all of our own design. They are direct results of how we think and act. For every action, there is a re-action. Simply put, we create our own environment and oftentimes without regard to possible outcomes. I have had many conversations with individuals who were in some way abusing their self who have stated the only person I am hurting is me. Nothing is further from the truth. Everything we do affects other people. We constantly transmit positive or negative to others or to ourselves. Each day we awake, we have the choice of living in Gods will (free) or self- will (manufactured and for sale).

Events of our past have nothing to do with the present moment. None of us lives in perfection yet we are perfect for God. God is hallowed and we are not. That which happened five minutes ago is history, which cannot be the present. Spirituality requires that we seek to do the next right thing. What is important is our intent. If we make a mistake, will we seek a better choice or will we continue doing the same thing expecting different results? Sadly, many choose the latter and more often than not, it is due to fear of the unknown. It is always the fear of letting go. Instead of asking our Creator for guidance, we think we should have the answers on our own. I fully believe I have kept God amused on many occasions. Left alone, I can be a dangerous man! It is healthy when we can look back and laugh at ourselves because we realize some of the things we do are plain dumb and comical. I also believe God, as any parent, enjoys having fun with His children. Likewise, He is always there to treat and care for us when we are in pain. Your life is a gift! Celebrate what you have, and tell your face about it. A warm smile goes a long way.

Self- will is a state of complete deception. It is a monster which feeds upon us until there is virtually nothing left. I had lived in this state for many years. I could describe it as being the chrome ball in a pin ball machine, bumping into all objects, bells ringing, lights flashing, falling down to the hammers to be struck or into nothingness, only to be re-cycled and go through the same process again and again. This is an analogy of living in self-will without all the gritty details. Perhaps you know of this from your own experiences. If not, I can tell you, it is not necessary that you visit this state of being to live upon a spiritual path. No matter how we get here, the important thing is that we arrive. I have known those who seem to have lived their lives in true Christianity and those who tried to have God co-sign their desires. I was once among the latter and it did not work. As painful as our situations may be, we will eventually learn to have gratitude, because they become a teaching tool and our greatest ally. The defeat by self-will drives us to seek free will or God's will. We become insistent upon finding the truth from what we knew as a world of lies. Again, most of these lies were of our own design, or what we told and felt about ourselves. Instead of truly seeking a solution, we judged ourselves in a most inhumane manner. We were playing God yet none of this is the role of His will for us.

Our minds speak to us but that does not mean we need to believe what it tells us. When we begin listening to our heart, progress begins. Unfortunately, many will believe the mind until death, whether it is of natural causes or perhaps suicide, which is a permanent solution to temporary problems. We can easily understand this is a very progressive condition, having lethal results. It happens every day. We should consider that every animal God created roams the earth freely. Yet, we build our own cages around ourselves, becoming incarcerated, all of which is a direct result of living in self-will. What so many fail to realize is the fact that we hold our very own key to freedom from bondage of self. How do we escape the tyranny? It is simple. Quit playing God and go to God as you are, at any given time of trouble. I am not saying this will get you out of a jail cell but it will get you out of your own self-created prison cell. I dedicated five years of Saturday afternoons taking a message to prison inmates and some of them actually found freedom, even though they remained behind bars. Those who found freedom sincerely desired a personal change. We cannot change our personalities unless we have principles to practice. It will not happen. This acquirement comes from being completely honest with ourselves, and our God. If your mind is telling you negative information, change the channel of your thinking. You have the ability and it is that simple.

Now that we come to see and understand the destruction and characteristics of living in self-will, the shame, guilt and remorse it instills upon us, I ask you now to look at the greatest of all reasons to change. Are we not denying the great fact that Christ died for our sins? This is a very uncomfortable concept yet it holds much truth. Jesus has forgiven you. There is no reason to continue torturing yourself and live within the walls of your own prison. Likewise, there is no reason to repeat the old patterns, the old acts or thoughts. We know what the results will be. The old life has to die that a new life will be born. Again, this is the demonstration of the resurrection of Christ. Are you willing to allow His death to be in vain? His complete teachings were of the natural laws and free will. What He offered to His followers was a choice and what He gave was promise, to gain entry into another dimension. This I know of today as heaven on earth. It is attainable by anyone and you will meet such people upon your path. "By their fruits, you will know them". If we come to fully understand this with clarity, we will witness our spiritual and oftentimes physical illnesses dissolve. Spiritual affects the physical. Many have fatal and progressive diseases which overtake them. What I have found is that, in God's hands, our fear of the outcome vanishes. I am fully confident that our passing will only be a transition into another realm. Just as all the changes we encounter in our lives here on earth, they are all transitions. We are born in free will, we grow into self-will and if we are lucky, we find ourselves seeking the simplicity of free will once again. We are born into innocence and to innocence we can return. It is a choice. God does not want you Holy. He wants you "healed".

No one possesses your answers, certainly not I. These you will find between yourself and your God. I would advise you to exercise caution should you encounter people who proclaim to being spiritual gurus. No one lives perfect lives and that is as it should be. We will make many mistakes on this plane, but it is the reckoning of our errors and the seeking of the truths that have such an incredible impact on our lives. It is when we sit in prayer and meditation that we make conscious contact with God. We ask Him to take all of us, good and bad, that these great changes take place in our personal lives. Some may view this as a recipe for a dull and boring life. To the contrary, it is only in this mentality that we live in full and in completeness. We will not always be in conscious contact with God but we should always put God foremost in what we do, how we think, how we act and react. The more we seek His will, the more we find ourselves growing out of self-will. It has been taught throughout the ages that we would know riches beyond our imaginations. This does not mean monetary gain, even though that may happen as well. What we find is that we acquire resources. In this case, our spiritual resources begin their growth. Our fear, guilt, shame, remorse judgments begin to leave us. We begin to live again with honor and newfound freedom. As we step away from our old self-designed lives, we find a new way of life that works. For many, it will be the first time of experiencing serenity.

As we begin to practice principles, we notice some very amazing and wonderful changes developing. We welcome the new as it feels and works much better. This in itself pushes us to desire more of that which we experience. We strive to become better individuals. We un-plug from ourselves and begin to plug into others as we realize we are all children of God. Our true purpose is to love and help one another. As we help another person we find that what we think to be our own problems seem less important. This gives us great purpose and God will not send anyone into your life that you cannot help in some way. Even if all you can do is be a good, can be of great importance. Over the years, I have had the honor of sharing with countless people. I never have their answers or tell them what they should or should not do. I simply share my own experiences of what worked and did not work in my personal life. To do anything more presents the possibility of affecting their own understanding as they venture their path. Looking at this honestly, they are most likely helping me more than I help them. It is the act of genuine care which keeps me grounded in principles. It is certainly amazing how this all works out. The more I give away freely, the more I attain. Even so, I give all credit to God. The highest achievement I will ever accomplish is to be a channel of His love and power. What a peaceful place this is to find oneself. What richness and a blessing this truly is. Why is it so magnificent? Because it is totally, free. There are no strings and no expectations. This is living within grace. In self will we create limitations, which restricts. In free will, we allow the unlimited. This is very simple and what I have found to be true.

2

Prayer and Meditation

The time we dedicate to pray and meditate is our highest personal activity performed. It is our time alone for conscious contact and to commune with God. As we can only demonstrate from where we are spiritually, in prayer and meditation, we are seeking further advancement in thought and action. We are in the process of building the soul. As we become still and quiet with our Creator, we open the channel to our higher self. Personally, I try to set aside at least twice a day and it is in two parts. In my waking hours I find myself in contemplation, and in the evening, in reflection. There have been times I have not been able to focus properly, and in my experience it is best to clear my mind and wait until I am able to be quiet inside. There is no right or wrong way and you should do what is comfortable for you. You do not have to be in a state of serenity to pray. This is your time alone with God and no one else is present. At this time, everything in your entire life is between you and Him. I have known many times that I would go days or perhaps even weeks when I could not feel the inner quietness and it was honestly all due to the fact that I would be plugged into self instead of God. However, my tolerance level for pain is not near what it once was.

What is it that actually happens when we pray? We are giving spiritual treatment to ourselves, to others or any given situation, often to areas that appear to be beyond our control. We are experiencing at the time the realm of love, which is infinite, all good, and serving. We may not realize it but we are allocating information to the subconscious that we are experiencing in the conscious. Perhaps more importantly, we are professing our lack of personal power and tapping into the Source of all power. We build our house or higher self upon this foundation. I have found that this is being in a state of absolution that I release to God who I am, where I am, and what I am. Perhaps I am seeking forgiveness or freedom from one sort of bondage of self or another. Whatever the case may be, I am coming to God as I truly am at the time, seeking His direction. When we give a situation to God that is exactly where we need to leave it. The outcome is none of our business. Other than living happy, joyful, I and free, I have no idea of what God's will is. It is vital we not merely think but rather we know and trust, and care is provided. This is faith; however faith requires effort on our part. More often than not, we find that the majority of the work is simply taking ourselves out of the way. We have heard many times, "let go and let God". As stated earlier, this is your time to commune; you should seek that which works best for you.

Over the years, I have come to know and appreciate the fact that God gives me not what I think I want but everything I really need. After some time I discovered my prayers became simpler as my faith developed. Certainly, I pray for other people and situations, but I know my needs are already granted. I ask to be an instrument, and a better individual. The rest is giving gratitude for what I have (that which has been freely given) and have not, (which I have yet to attain). With this awareness, I have no wants. Every step of our paths yields the new, the fresh. We do well to take time to breathe it in and experience the moments and be with them. If we hurry, we risk missing an experience which may be monumental. Likewise, with prayer, if we do not show up, we have most likely missed out. It is a simple matter of action and reaction. Here again we have the choice of living today in discord, (self-will), or in harmony with the universe, (God's will).

Meditation, as in prayer, requires concentration or thought. We come into a state of reflection and introspection. In short, we are giving consideration to where we are spiritually at a given time. Perhaps some incident that happened years ago and brought us pain has resurfaced. Perhaps our thoughts are of something that makes us very happy in the present moment. Whatever the case may be, it is time to be with it and acknowledge it. It is a time to treat the feeling in a healing manner or treat ourselves in a joyous state as a wonderful present. Life itself is a myriad of events to experience. It is by claiming the comfort and discomfort that we find a balance in emotions. Far too many people focus too much on the discord. Reckoning the joy of living dissolves pain and demonstrates gratitude to our Creator. The loss of a loved one will certainly bring about a feeling of grief that is overwhelming. This is of the spiritual world and we will eventually heal as we remember the joy and importance they have brought us. Just as birth is a transition, it is also true with death. It may take a great deal of time but with God's care, we will return to a balance. The loss of items in the material world is replaceable. The material goods you have acquired have nothing to do with your spiritual self. It is in the latter that we find our true wealth or riches, which reach into infinity. There are many gifts that wait, which are far beyond our present comprehension. The attainment is solely dependent upon that which we allow ourselves. Our Creator wants us to have these gifts and the only block is ourselves.

As the gravity of earth bounds our physical bodies, our spiritual selves are free to travel anywhere we wish or summon to our consciousness. It is unlimited because we are allowing our higher self's freedom of what we think is finite to commune with our Creator, who is infinite. In meditation, we are actually released from all physical and mental bondage. Perhaps you or someone you know is afflicted with a disabling disease or handicap. Does this mean their spirit is limited? I would argue that this is far from the truth. Even in the case where one's brain is not functioning properly or even at all, does this mean their spirit is exhausted? Medical science may tell us this is so, but who are we to say? Let us take a moment to consider another avenue. We have heard many times of" turning our will and our lives over to the care of God". This means exactly what it says. The ability to transfer both will and life is inside of you. Most likely, you have performed this many times, unaware of its power. Let us say, for example, someone comes to you with a situation which has brought them severe depression and they can see no possible solution. You look into your own heart, and with love, you offer them words of encouragement, hope, and perhaps your own experience. What is actually happening is you are extending to them, through God, your own will and love. They borrow from you what they lack and need at present. You can exercise this ability at any time or in any situation, even if the subject person has left this life.

The purpose of the above paragraph should serve as a simple cornerstone in meditation. For that which you give to your Creator, He has vested power in you. Meditation, being a state of awareness, it is important we acknowledge our wealth, where it comes from and how we may pass it along to others. By doing so, we are giving growth to our present and future abilities and our understanding. By this exercise, we find that our following prayers develop more accurately and purposefully defined. There is no right or wrong way to meditate and pray. The most important factor is to begin. The very first step you take is the most important of all the footprints you will leave behind. Allow this to be your first thought of each of your days and you will do just fine. Place your thoughts upon making simple progress. The remaining appears as you become prepared to receive. Enjoy the days of bounty, as there will surely be times we will put on a suit of armor and wrestle with the angels all day long. We are not going to live perfect lives. I have been on this earth fifty-eight years and about one third of that has been dedicated to living on a spiritual path. There have been times when I have had to fold my hands, times that I was completely lost and even times that I was angry with God. The only way I have ever found my way out of those times was to show up to Him exactly where I was in any given situation or period of my life. To show up was my key and it took me years to absorb that simple fact. Very few apparent spiritual changes will occur unless we are consciously present and participating in our own life.

Whether realized or not, there is a perfect design and purpose for your being. We may go our complete time here without understanding what it may entail, yet it is there in our existence. On a personal level, my destiny is none of my business. As I ask God to utilize me as an instrument, how could it be any other way? I fully believe that every experience handed to me has reason. I may not understand it, I may refuse it for a time, it may bring comfort or pain whatever the case may be, and I am destined to experience it. God consciousness is a river

forever flowing, going to some destination and shaping everything in its path. Unlike a still pond, which has debris at the
bottom, which decomposes and remains there, the current of
a river is always moving matter to another location. Perhaps
this is why we sometimes feel as though we are homesick for
some place we have never been before. In the spirit world,
we move into the current in which we feed. What you may
not realize is that the river also feeds upon you. This is true as
what goodness we are given, we freely give away to another
and it passes on like the rushing water.

In meditation and prayer, allow yourself to be a river. Living
in self-will is like a still pond, it becomes stagnant and decomposes. It becomes part of a floor, which supports a mass
of weight. As you sit in quietness, acknowledge where you
are, where you wish to go, and what stands in your way. Ask
for removal of the obstacle and allow it to happen. God has
never taken away from me anything I wished to hold on to
and the only obstacle that is ever in my way, is I. The solution
is always the same, change those things we are capable of,
and place what we cannot change in God's hand and trust
that it is in the proper place. Here, we find a simple recipe for
building our faith. It requires a great deal of courage to face
ourselves. All who possess faith also possess courage. I have
found it most helpful to face myself in meditation before I
begin my prayer time. It helps to know what we need to pray
for, what are our weaknesses, and what strengths we have
available. Utilize the strength vested unto you. If you are one
of those who turn every situation in your life over to God and
are not providing the footwork, it may be a certain sign of
slothfulness.

Over time, the things I prayed for myself began to dwindle
as I realized my shortcomings had much less power. There

is a great reason for that and it is because I kept showing up to God. I certainly kept making mistakes but I became more conscious of my thinking and actions. Somewhere along the line I began to give much more consideration to what I may do for God, not that He needs my help with a single matter, but there was a change in course that evolved and I had only very little to do with it. I had not thought myself into an honorable life; I had lived my life into honorable thinking. By the grace of God, this evolved.

3

Gratitude

I attend spiritual discussion groups on a regular basis. Presently it is near Christmas and gratitude is always a major topic during the holidays. I find great joy in listening to others express all they have in their life for which they are grateful. The birth, the life, and the teachings of Christ, are of the most importance. This I acknowledge in each daily meditation, for without it I would have no design for living. We give gratitude for our lives and the experiences, families, loved ones and friends, our homes, food and clothing. When we consciously consider our gifts, we find they are countless. I have a mate who possesses a more tenderness of heart than any human I have known. We have a wonderful daughter who has dedicated her life to helping others as a Doctor of Psychology, for which I hold amazement and the deepest of admiration and gratitude. She is such a beautiful person, inside and out. I am very well blessed. My gratitude list would consist of many pages.

As I dwell upon all that I have, I find that perhaps I have more gratitude for what I have not. I do not have the right or desire to judge any other being. I do not have the answers to anyone's life problems; to pretend to may distract them from what God has planned for their life. I know only a little of the spiritual realm as this leaves me teachable and open to learn. I do not have a view of the big picture; rather I receive pieces of the puzzle as I walk upon my path. I do not have knowledge of what you should or should not do; all of your experiences are, intended especially for you. I can only share with you my own experience, strength and hopes. I have no relationships in my life which are possessive. We are all free and wandering spirits. I do not have or desire to hold the destiny of my own life. I placed that in God's hands years ago and He is doing with it much better than I am capable. I have found that what I do not have also sustains me. In a different realm of thought and actions, it is here that I find my balance with the universe. I can move between separate realities with unlimited boundaries or I can center upon daily life on this planet with all the perfections and imperfections. I have found this shifting process occurs during my meditations. It is a time I seem to step outside of my physical body and look inside of my spiritual state, however it may be at any given time. It is a time that I am completely alone with God. It has taken me years to acquire this state and the main purpose is to clear my own perception. Certainly, I consider my complete environment and life upon this earth, but how I perceive all matters is of the greatest importance. I come to my Creator with clear eyes and open heart. Should I feel discord in any area of my life, my own perception is the first thing I look at.

Gratitude is not just a thought or feeling. It is an action and, as we know, every action has re-action. Over the years, I have had people show up in my life who were facing problems of a wide variety or they may have needed to have someone to hear their concerns. I instantly have gratitude for the fact that they trust me enough to come to me in the first place, and then I focus upon how I may be of help and put it into action. As I stated earlier, God is not going to send anyone into our lives that we cannot help. Maybe they need transportation to go to their job. Maybe they need food, clothes, or shelter. Maybe they have lost their hope. Whatever the case may be, I find gratitude that I care enough to be of assistance. I am grateful that God trusted in me enough to send these people into my life. Anytime we extend a helping hand or even an ear, gratitude becomes an action. Gratitude is also an entity which holds much power. It is complete within itself. It is up to us whether it is only a pleasant emotion or if it is an action. I have had those who come to me with their deepest and darkest secrets and as I listen to them a chain of events unfolds. First, the person has verbalized their secret, therefore it has already lost much of its power over them, I do not have their answer but I can share my own experience so they do not feel alone. Last but most important, the situation being treated with gratitude is placed in God's hands which is the solution. As you can see, all I have done was be a channel. Yet they walk away with some measure of relief from some horrible bondage. I thank God for being of service and the deal is complete. There is nothing for me to take credit for and I have nothing to do with the outcome. Gratitude has fulfilled itself.

Gratitude in action always means moving forward in the practice of principles. To me, being in a state of gratitude is magical. I have found that the possibilities and effects are endless. I have dwelled upon the definitions of the word but the actual effect far supersedes its definition. Personally, I have found it to be in a state of complete agreement with God's will, whatever that may be. It is the essence of hope. It calls upon and challenges my level of faith. It demonstrates my lack of power alone, but through God I become vested with such abilities.

As I consider this, I have to think of the serenity prayer, which is very simple, but complete. "God grant me the serenity to accept the things I cannot change, the courage to change the things I can, and the wisdom to know the difference". The first section we are admitting that alone we are powerless. Often I have found that all I can really change is my perception of situations. In this simple sentence, I am also asking for freedom from any form of self-will. I have no motives and there is no self-seeking. The second part, we are asking for courage to change the matters we are capable. It requires great courage to honestly look deep inside ourselves and admit the character flaws we possess. It takes time and a great deal of effort but the power vested in us by God gives us courage to make changes in our life. Therefore, the power to change is available. As I stated earlier to simply dump all our problems on God and sit back and wait for changes to appear may be disappointing. This is sloth. It is our responsibility to do the footwork and for each of us, there is much work ahead. The last part of the Serenity Prayer is for our knowledge from our Creator to know what is beyond our personal power. We cannot change all the insanities of humankind on this earth but as we make individual changes, we are making the earth a better place to exist. As we pass along the wisdom that we have found to our fellows, this is an act of gratitude. As in a parent /child relationship, we wish for them a healthy, wholesome, and more productive experience. Yet we know we cannot and should not attempt to mold them to any specifications. We give what we can and pray for their wellbeing.

Gratitude is an unlimited source of gifts that we may give to each other. There are fourteen hundred and forty minutes in each day. Have you taken one of those minutes to give thanks for what you have? As with meditation and prayer, gratitude opens the door to the kingdom. At any time I freely give of myself to another, without conditions or strings attached, I find my own personal freedom soaring. I have no power in the outcome but I usually find it has positive results. Again, I have only served as a channel for God's will to occur. I have found that this is my place and that which brings me comfort and sanity on this earth. Any time I am in the presence of gratitude my soul is in alignment with the universe.

Of all the spiritual tools we have available, gratitude is our greatest healer. It allows us to treat others and ourselves with unconditional love and respect. I have found that anytime I am not in a state of gratitude, I am into some degree of self-will. I have those times still today and probably always will. For a long time I would be upset with myself during these times but eventually I learned that I was about to receive a lesson in humility. So as painful as those times may be, they are necessary for our growth. Conceit cannot exist within a truthful and fully thankful heart. It is impossible. Gratitude as I would define it is out- going love. Short, simple and yet complete. There is no room for anything of selfish designs. It is self-less.

It is also from gratitude that we earn our honor. Perhaps that is all we really have. We do not take anything with us when we leave this earth. We can only leave behind our memories, our respect, integrity and dignity as we consider what a privilege it has been to walk upon this earth with all our experiences. These of course are dependent upon what we do and how we live our lives today. As I write this, I think about my grandfather who passed away many years ago. He was the main figure in my life and the person who took up most of his time with me. Although he was the simplest of men, he was the most spiritual man I have ever known. I never knew of him to make a negative remark about anyone. Everything he did projected love, tolerance, and patience. He has always remained my hero. All that I learned from him remained with me. Even in times of my own spiritual destitution his character and morality remained with me. Perhaps this was why some of my times were so painful. I had a head load of his decency as I strayed far away from any realm of spiritual living. His memory eventually guided me back to the path that I walk today. His demonstrations spoke for himself. He was and remains the most noblest of men I have ever known. It was not so much as what he taught me verbally; rather, how he lived his life was an inspiration. I hope to sit and talk with him again when I transcend from this life.

Your own worthiness is wide, deep, and travels far. Never underestimate the power of living upon a spiritual plane. It serves much more than you realize. It gives long after your physical existence. Have patience in your development as these matters happen in God's time and not ours, but they will surely come provided we keep seeking the truths of life. Living spiritually is very simple but it is not easy. You will find many challenges along your way. Try to find gratitude in these times, as they are our teachers. Much of our old attitudes and outlooks we have to unlearn in order for the new to take place. It takes time, and we do well not to rush. Your reward will be internal peace for all time, which is priceless. It remains inside wherever you go and whatever you do. You become a mirror that reflects all that is good and healthy. The principle we obtain and reflect unto others is our primary reason for existence.

I have found that my gratitude derives from facing my greatest fear, which is my own self. It is only after I truly face my emotional deformities I realize what I must work on. Admission is the very first step toward freedom from our own enslavement. Again, this is of self-creation we have produced in forgiving our pain but find that we have yet to heal the remaining scars. We must completely release them in order to gain our true freedom. We find that we simply cannot afford to hold on to the destructive patterns of the past. It is gone and has no place in the present moment. I spent many years attempting to wish past pain away and it never worked but when I came to the point I could accept and simply am with what I was feeling, the power these matters had over me began to melt away. When I would arrive on the other side of these feelings I would have gratitude for the lessons they had taught me. The results have always been the same; when I changed the way I look at things, the things I looked at changed. How amazingly simple, yet it works every time!

TIME: It took me a great deal of time to appreciate the gratitude in life today. I chose many undesirable paths before I found the right one that worked for me. I love to sit by rivers and watch the waters rushing by me. I like to watch the rhythmic pattern of the swells as the current shifts by some object underneath that I do not see. If I am lucky, I may see a rainbow trout surface for only a second and display an instant array of colors. I love walking the shores inspecting thousands of finely polished pebbles that are colorful, beautiful, and unique that before were boulders that time and force have created. I love looking into the sky on a clear night at all the amazing stars that were once planets which burned out, yet we still see their light. Even though they are so very far away, light-years later we still see the reflection of what once was. These very things make me think of time itself. The past are today's memories and tomorrows are today's dreams. Allow today to be what you long for your future. It is time that has carved my life from the different currents and pressures of *every experience* I can possibly remember and my hopes for any *tomorrows* I may know. If I can see glimmers of light thousands of years old and only have fleeting glimpses of the future, there is no division of time, for it is endless. I can only exist in the current moment.

What does this have to do with gratitude? Time has everything to do with gratitude! It is the design and creation of The Great Grandfather and His perfection. It shapes us just as the softness of water shapes the hardness of rock. As small as we may be, we are all a part of the grand scheme of things. You are meant to be here. Perhaps we are only in a beginning stage here on earth. If you can acknowledge that a worm can transform into a beautiful butterfly, a diamond created from coal, there is no reason or proof that man will not and cannot evolve into something much greater than we can presently comprehend. If we have gratitude for our shaping here and now, we are linear with God's will for us whatever that may be. I have no idea what that may entail. All I know is that I have faith and that alone will lead me to wherever I need to go. God and you, as a reader and seeker every second of each day, accompany me on my own journey. Not only do I have much gratitude, I have a very deep respect. Love your journey.

The world may be a troubled place to exist with its current situations but in case no one has told you, if you tap into The Power, you have the ability to change the world. How is this possible when we are in fact the *powerless*? Because it is only you who can live your own life and it is changeable at any time one may choose. How wonderful it is to have the ability to shift consciousness of our perplexed minds into praying for the next right thing to do. The fact is we can change the world anytime we wish or need to. We cannot save the world but we can definitely change it.

4

An Inside Job

The complete teachings of Jesus were instruction on how to attain our higher selves, how to live in harmony and what we must do in order for life in the spirit world to take place. It appears to have been His singleness of purpose. There is absolutely nothing to argue of His teachings nor was there anything left out. He made clear that there was a design for living well for all humankind. God does not have favorites. Never has, never will. In the years of my own personal studies and experiences, I became aware that all that Jesus taught was on an individual level. I believe this is not only remarkable but also imperative that we understand. There are no barriers in His teachings. There are no chosen people. Regardless of race, religions, or any other matter, the teachings apply to every human. In fact, it does not require any religion at all. It is certain that humankind has warped and distorted His teachings. As we see and consider these distortions, it is clear to see where man has attempted to change the course of the natural laws to benefit themselves. These distortions we shall eventually recognize to be the work of robbers and thieves of culture. Here I am defining culture as a way of life. They want or claim to live a spiritual lifestyle but they have not done or attempted the mandatory footwork in order for this to be a truth of their being. They say one thing but act as another. They are divided or inconclusive as to how they choose to live their lives. I am not expressing judgment here but what I am stating is the fact that the only way to turn your will and life over to the care of God, is to do exactly that. There is no middle of the road solution. Either we do it or we do not.

I cannot express enough the fact that any mistake one has ever made, forgiveness has taken place if we have sincerely asked. We have all bared our battle scars and now we must finally rid ourselves of them. To face and claim these mistakes is mandatory, however. Our intent must be to give all of ourselves to God, leaving nothing out. Perfection does not exist within this realm, but rather we strive for progress to take place. I cannot tell you how many times I have meditated and entered prayer with: You know God I am one strange individual. I felt that He was finding laughter, and later on down the road I could share that laughter with Him. This was also a great turning point in my life. I did not take myself seriously any longer. Why should I? I am not running the show any longer, nor do I wish too. This is one of the many facets of my life I cannot afford to fool myself about.

So how do we go about this inner cleansing? We embark upon a fact-finding and fact-facing mission of our own history. This is a very simple concept but it can be very difficult to perform. It is very helpful to remember that God loves you enough to allow you to try to run your own life. We set pen to paper and reflect upon those people we have hurt, have judged, those we have resented for some act they may have done to us, or how we have perceived them. We look at all areas where we have been dishonest, that we created jealously, guilt, shame, and remorse. We look at everything we have done or said that has been harmful to others. We consider our deepest and darkest secrets we have vowed never to allow another human know about. We must look at how our actions or words have affected these people and realize what part of them we affected. Was it their love, trust, honor, dignity, or ethics that we damaged? It is vital that we be honest and thorough here because it is only here that we begin to be free ourselves. The idea here is to clean our own house. It is here we begin to emerge from the darkness and feel the sunlight of the spirit on our faces. Very little grows in the dark. If we are thorough, we have faced some large portions of truth about ourselves that we can clearly see upon the paper listing our shortcomings.

Next, we refer back to our list of people we have harmed and begin to make our amends whenever possible. We may find them to be receptive and sometimes they may continue their anger toward us. The important thing is that we have admitted these matters to God and tried to clean our side of the fence with those individuals. It is also important to understand that we should not go to these people if doing so would create more harm. I cannot clear my conscious at the expense of another. Those matters I take to God and some other individual I completely trust. This is a hard but extremely important task. No one likes to admit his or her own faults, but we must if we wish to grow and become free. Keep your pen and paper handy, as there will be other matters which may arise later that we had forgotten about or they may be new. Whatever the case may be, we need to apply the same method of treatment as quickly as we realize them.

Our secrets are what restrains us from spiritual growth or keeps us in illness. It is only common sense that the deeper the secret the deeper the personal conflicts will exist. Our development requires work and faith. The above matters do not simply go away. They require attention and action. If we leave something out, we are only shortchanging ourselves. Holding onto anything of the past defies or restricts the present moments in your life which are fresh and new. What an absolute miracle it is to begin each day in this fashion. Before I go to sleep each night, I meditate the events of the day and have prayer time. When I awake, it is in the same manner. I ask for guidance for the day and bear witness to the miracles I see and experience. Within this habit, I find very little, if any, upsets in life. It does not mean that they have not come or will not continue to come but today I know how to handle these situations. I give up my powerlessness to the One who holds all power and I leave it there. It is very simple and effective.

The internal cleansing process may be a very emotional and painful ordeal. Unfortunately, we must go through it to get to our goal, which is spiritual freedom. However, the benefit we shall reap is well worth any discomfort the process may bring. When I first truly faced myself, and all that I had done that resulted in my shame, guilt, fear, and remorse, I thought it would actually kill me. I knew that it had to come out if I were to receive any form of closure to the pain I carried. I recall performing this ritual with a minister, which was also uncomfortable, as I had never spoken with one before. I have never belonged to any type of organized religion. I remember asking him before we started if he needed to take a valium or something. He laughed but I was serious. I really felt bad for him being on the receiving end of what I would confess to him. I am happy to say we both survived it. Then something amazing happened. I began to cry and I cried for three days and nights non- stop. Afterward, I began to feel my freedom emerge from some hidden place. Many know this as a spiritual experience. It was the very first time I had felt the presence of God. This was my own cleansing I had to experience. On the fourth night, I slept like a baby. Both my relief and release had finally come and I realized for the first time that God actually exists. I had been with Him. It was only a beginning and all I had was a small amount of willingness.

We cleanse ourselves from the inner to the outer. We are never alone with this task. It takes time, work and patience. After a time we find that our dignity and self-respect begins to return. We begin to learn humility that is essential for spiritual development. The old experiences that bound us in negativity were only teaching experiences. They should no longer have control over you. They served a very meaningful purpose but they are history. Anything that arrives in your life today that causes discord, look at it, be with it, see what it is teaching, and then let it go. Let it go back into the realm from which it came and that is usually our own minds. This is where all of our discord is produced. God does not send confusion into our lives; we create it ourselves. This is the voice of our lower selves. In order to attain our higher selves we need to listen, look, and feel from the depths of our hearts. Here is where we find the truths of our existence. We sort through what did and did not work. In short, we take a complete inventory of ourselves, and release that which does us harm. It is equally important to be aware of that which is and will become the good, as given from our Creator, and we should be grateful for the many gifts we have received. We find that the more energy we put into our work the greater the gifts become. The deeper we look inside the more clarity is revealed.

The greatest achievement I am aware of is when God places a new person in my life, coming to me in trust and desiring to share their pain and problems. I do not pat myself on the back but rather give credit and thanks to God, which is the source of all that may be helpful to another within me. Without this order in my life, I am nothing. This order does not come by what I think but what I do. When I consider these people who show up in my life I realize they are probably helping me more than I am helping them. I get the opportunity to share more of my innermost heart-felt thoughts. These people are miracles that appear and I am privileged and grateful to share these moments. These are moments to demonstrate a channel of Thy love and Thy power. There is nothing more fulfilling or no greater honor. My personal life has risen from a state of complete hopelessness to times I have felt I have walked through two giant pillars into freedom, and yet I realize there is so much more to be done. I have only scratched the surface and feel I am like a single grain of sand blowing in a desert wind. This is how small I am. I love the desert wind as it has blown on my face and through my hair so many times before. I am content being a grain of sand with no known destiny. What an incredible journey. I would not change anything about it.

The stability in my life today comes from what I give rather than what I receive. Yet one does not happen without the other. I have come to know this as life in balance. Like any scale, easily tipped depending on how much we place upon each platform, it is our own obligation to maintain balance. Here balance is defined as to" keep in place". That of yesterday served its purpose but now it is today. You learned something yesterday of how to better live in the present moment. On a spiritual plane, we are constantly giving and receiving. We are taking in and we are giving out. We are allowing all our experiences to flow through us. What we find questionable or harmful to our well-being, we release and focus on the next right thing. If we see how any of our thoughts or actions may have brought harm to another being, we must immediately take the required corrective measures. This is required maintenance to remain in emotional sobriety. How do we gain this achievement? It is a direct result of placing all our faith unto God. We have found this is what works when nothing else will. For our efforts we are rewarded a degree of humility.

It has taken a great deal of courage to face ourselves as we really are. Later on, we realize that very little growth would occur had we not set upon this fact-finding mission. Once again, we find that what was so dreaded became a strong ally as it relieves us from bondage of our own thinking. Our complete weaknesses center in our minds. This is what we really wish to escape. This is the virtual prison we build for ourselves.

5

Miracles

As we venture into our cleansing, (which is a lifelong process), it becomes clear that our problems are of our own design. We created the lifestyle in which we have lived. Likewise, we are the only ones who can live ourselves out of its bondage. No one can do it for you. Certainly, psychologists, psychiatrists, or perhaps clergy may be of great assistance, but this is a trek we must make ourselves. The only way this is accomplished is through God and our higher selves. We must completely change our thinking. That requires that our old pattern of thought must die. We cannot think of God and discord at the same time. It is impossible. We can be into either our lower self or our higher self but we cannot be in the same space at the same time. We can no more do this than we can be in New York and Arizona at the same moment. It is imperative to understand this fact. At any given time, we are what we *think* we are. God, does not judge or punish us, we do this to ourselves. This is the reason why each morning that I go to God I ask that He accept *all* of me, good and not so good, strength and weakness. With this simple and short prayer, I have opened a door for miracles to take place in not only my life but also the lives of those I meet every day. This is my great payday; I get to see the miracles God has performed within the eyes of other people and it brings me great joy and inner peace.

As I mentioned in the chapter on gratitude, I attend group meetings daily that are spiritual in nature. They always end with The Lord's prayer. Quite a few years ago I stopped bowing my head and closing my eyes. This is in no way disrespect to God but rather there are three specific reasons that I keep my eyes open and look into the faces of others. One, I believe God thinks I bowed my head far too long in life. Two, this is how I see God in physical form, and third, this is how I see angels. You are not going to see angels unless you are looking for them. It is a fact that I am in the presence of God, surrounded by miracles and angels every day. This came to me by simply changing my point of view and perception. When we are in our *higher selves,* we have the ability to step inside the phenomenon many call grace. It is a place with abundance of possibilities, unlimited source and potential. It is a place where all your true riches are stored yet you cannot count them. Why would one waste their time? Opposite of the material world, these are riches you cannot fully *give* away. Along your spiritual path, there may come times when one feels they have given everything they have but the human soul is incredible. There is always more to give as the soul constantly replenishes itself. What an amazing process this is. The reality is this. God is working in your life, within everyone else, and in mine. All that is required is that we choose firmly and as honestly as possible. With only the slightest amount of willingness, a door opens that we may pass through as free people if we put forth effort.

God does not want you holy He wants you healed. He has the

holy department under control. I do not believe He cares how we come to Him as long as we simply show up. There are, however, holy people who walk this earth and I have had the fortune of knowing some of them. If they were not here, we would know nothing of holiness, as they demonstrate to us far greater avenues of living well than we could realize on our own. I have strong ties to Native American culture by blood and beliefs. My belief system itself is all I truly possess. Everything else is of the material world in which I have very little concern. I will leave this earth with only footprints of where I have been. I have nothing more and nothing less than my own personal experiences. Those are priceless. For many years, I felt I had been born centuries before or I was born far too late. My outlook on society as we know today did not blend very well. I remember not long after I found myself in defeat someone told me "the world is in perfect order; you just do not understand it." I thought that perhaps he was right and I dwelled upon that for a long time. My serenity is dependent upon my acceptance. I could even see that to a point. At some point along my own spiritual path, it became clear to me that this was not always true. I do not have to agree with what goes on in society and have every right to reject that which is harmful to others and to me. I did have the realization that I did not possess the power to change the world but I could change the effects society had upon me. This was a magnificent revelation because it took me from looking away from the outer reality into the inner reality. I no longer felt I needed to buy into that which society was selling. I no longer had to participate in the realm of my old thinking and questions of what I truly believed. Here was another miracle. I was able to eventually find my innermost self that had been deranged, damaged and lost for so long. I had long been away from the principles I actually had inside for the sake of fitting into something I never needed to begin with. This was my mistake, my downfall, and my ultimate defeat. I had not allowed God to be the center of my universe, instead I had chosen other people's acceptance and that failed me.

Insanity, as I have known it, is seemingly a horrible place to be. Yet, had I not become completely lost I may have never found myself again. It is the tragic price of living in self-will. Had I not had the years and experiences of suffering through alcoholism and drug addiction, I would probably not have sought God in the manner I have for many years now. When I dwell upon this, I can have no regret for the past. It is quite clear I hurt other people and I have made amends to them all to the best of my ability. Had I not known hopelessness I could not have comprehended grace. If not been beaten down from self-will, I would not know selflessness. Had I not been a taker, I could not be a real giver. Today I am grateful for all of my experiences. I welcome weakness just as much as I welcome strength because it helps me to realize that spiritual living is a lifelong process. I celebrate the joy of living each day as I extend myself to another. The highest achievement I will ever attain is to be a messenger, and really, that is a simple job; all I can do is take someone to the message. Again, God does not want us holy; He wants us healed. He and Jesus have the holy department fully under control.

I do not just believe in miracles, I depend on them. If for whatever reason you do not see them there is a great chance you simply have your eyes closed. If you are not living a life that is happy, joyous, and free, you are cheating yourself. Long ago, there was a man that told me that when I pass from earth and personally meet God, He would have only one question for me; and that is "did you enjoy the life I gave you?" If you cannot answer, **YES** and **THANK YOU**, you may want to look at that. God has a tremendous sense of humor also. If you do not believe that, consider the fact that He created Gary Watson. Just as all children bring great laughter and joy, we are no different at all. I am certain that I brought Him many hearty belly laughs in my time. I am just as sure of that as I am the fact that He has been with me in my deepest pain and sorrow. Enjoy your miracles. They are entirely free even if you feel you have paid dearly. You will always find you set a price upon yourself. Alleviate your pain of the past by living in the present moment where your care is available. Find that thought that you can hang onto. Think of God who has been with you thus far and will be into eternity, for He is the Alpha and the Omega.

6

Faith

Faith is commitment, which must be with us at all times, else will we perish. It is our dedication, trust, and reliance upon our Creator. It is also our duty to allow ourselves to be present in what sometimes seems to be living in another dimension. Our faith is in line with our allegiance to demonstrate the miracles that occur, as we know them. This is the single most important part of a spiritual foundation that we build on for the rest of our life and retreat to on a daily basis. Each waking hour and the last thought I have each day is the devotion to that which keeps me alive and well in heart and spirit. Complete trust is always present in the life I live today. This matter is one of which I was in short supply for many years. I remember having to borrow the faith of others in order to build my own structure. It was through others I found my own faith and remarkable changes began to develop, even though they came slow at the time. I had to take a chance. One thing that I did realize however was the fact that if I did not take a chance, I did not have a chance. This is by far the single most important choice I have ever made in my lifetime.

What I was so desperately lacking during this era became fertile soil in which my soul would take deep root and grow to blossom. I have come to understand that faith is my daily resurrection. Each day is fresh, filled with opportunities, possibilities, and miracles. As it turned out, my personal surrender had been the key to a gateway. I had to come to a point that I ceased fighting everyone and everything, especially myself. It was only after beginning the task of getting self out of the way that I could seek God's will for me. It was a slow process but bit by bit, I began to learn a little about humility. Time and practice is our greatest healer. I had great knowledge and experience of what had not worked in the past but now I was standing on new ground and it felt good. Life does not come with a set of blueprints but I found a set of principles that worked under any conditions. I am a reasonably happy man and although my life is serene for the most part, I realize that I cannot become complacent. There are situations that will arise in the affairs of each of our lives. Sometimes they may be staggering. It is these times in particular that we need to look deep inside ourselves and summon all the courage we have. We can easily fall into fear, anger, guilt, and remorse or we can view them as a personal challenge. God does not test us, we test ourselves. If this were not true, why would we need faith? Faith is the most important growth tool we will ever know. Your faith affects every facet of your life. It is a measure of our alignment with God and the universe. It is also a vital key to our acceptance.

Suppose we fall short or for some reason temporarily lose our faith, what then? I can only share with you that the greatest lessons I have learned derived from my lack of faith. It was *always* because I was in self-will. I am very grateful that my awareness has honed me to a point I am able to see myself drifting off course. My Creator will allow me to try to run the show anytime I choose. However, my tolerance level for pain has drastically reduced over the years. I clearly remember the years of my own active addictions and I will explain it in this manner: I weigh about one hundred and sixty pounds and it was as if I would be walking into the ring with a professional heavyweight boxer. I would hit the floor immediately. Yet, armed with the knowledge I would continue the same behaviors repeatedly. I was fighting a battle that not one single man has ever won. This is only a brief description of the insanity of "self-will run riot". It is true with *all* addictions, be it alcohol, drugs, sex, gambling, power, or anything else one could imagine. The teaching of Christ, "knock and it shall be opened" remains undisputed. Faith is always just a thought and action away.

No matter how much effort we apply to our spiritual development we are going to make mistakes and become overwhelmed by situations. This is the nature of the human experience. We are all going to have our fragile moments. What matters is how we utilize these teachings of life and how we demonstrate that entrusted to us. I am not a very social creature by nature and there are many different reasons for this of which I am aware, and there are some things about my life where I am simply content. In my circle of living, I have the honor to do a great deal of one on one sharing with other individuals and in groups. As I stated earlier, I never have anyone's answers or have any desire to tell them what they should or should not do. I do not commiserate with anyone but I listen and share in empathy. I always thank God for the honor, as I am simply a medium to hear their concerns, hopes, and dreams and that is *all* that I am. I do not claim anything for myself but I do claim that God sometimes chooses me to be at a given place at a given time to be available. What more could I possibly wish for? Whether realized or not He, works through every one of us. I believe it important that we stake claim in our abilities granted, for they are all of God.

I have a fatal lung disease, (end stage emphysema). A little over a year ago I had two lung surgeries my pulmonary doctors wanted to try before placing me on a lung transplant list. The surgeries were not successful and brought no positive results. I was counseled about lung transplant two years ago. I was informed that without a transplant I would have twelve to twenty four months of life. I have faith in medical science; however I have more faith in God. The twenty-four months have passed and I am still here. I have not had a single second that I have fallen into self-pity concerning my situation. I did however have some frustration with the transplant center. I had first met with the transplant team, which included the pulmonary doctor, surgeon, and psychiatrist and shared with them my history. They put me through a battery of tests and later rejected me because I lacked a strong support team for post-surgery and because I once admitted myself to a psychiatric hospital for depression. I told them this up front and could not understand why they did not disqualify me from the beginning before going through the expense of testing. The decision of the psychiatrist was the matter that baffled me. I felt, in short, that he made a decision that people do not change. I realize the center carefully screens candidates and I made the conscious decision to forget about the matter and leave the outcome in God's hands. I came to easily rest with the thought that someone else will receive the new lungs I may have received with far greater ability of spiritual demonstration than I. I do not allow my physical condition to interfere with my spiritual intentions.

Because of faith, I have no fear of a final transition. I do not know if indeed it is final or not. Perhaps it is only the beginning of some other existence. I do know that I have lived a full life with an incredible amount of blessings. I have experienced much of heaven walking upon my path and appreciating my findings along the way. I also have to believe that if He granted me these wonderful gifts on this plane, it is quite possible plans exist for a further destiny. Faith may not have opened the doors of heaven and let me in but it definitely opened the gates of hell and let me walk out. I am truly grateful for *all* my experiences. I can look God in the eye and say yes, I enjoyed the life you give me. My life has consisted of revelations and demonstrations, which all arrived right on time. I lived myself out of a virtual prison into a life of wealth that cannot be purchased with any sum of money.

For years, I looked to God for forgiveness only to find that He never condemns us in the first place. Therefore, forgiveness has to come from within ourselves. Our character flaws, whether self-designed, (which is usually the case), or somehow inflicted upon us, can begin to be corrected with the help of our Creator. The Bible contains many beautiful stories concerning faith. In each story is a commonality among the characters; they all had to face themselves completely, including their doubts and fears. This requires great courage and, as we know, all who possess faith possess courage. The two are inseparable. Faith is our daily bread. Just as we need air, sun, food, and water, faith is the necessary nourishment for the soul to survive and flourish. Our souls can flow from this moment forward upon the bedrock like that of a river, touching many as it moves toward its destination. I believe it to be the incoming and out-going of love in its purest form. We normally do not see the impact we may have upon others by listening and sharing with empathy, yet we are feeding unto other individuals who are seeking their own nourishment. What a blessing it truly is to be a part of this chain. For it is here we come to realize the simplicity of our purpose, which is to be a mere instrument of the Greatest Power of All.

Many people will be very reluctant to turn their will and lives over to the care of God. This is the great leap of faith. I have no doubt at all that He is doing far much better at running my life than I could ever dream. I found that complete surrender was the pathway to strength and spiritual understanding. I began a thorough moral inventory of my life thus far and it was not a very nice picture. It was after I had completed a fact-finding effort that I stood naked before God in emotions. I asked that He take all of me just as I was. What followed was changes began to take place and miracles became apparent and I could clearly see these were part of a phenomenon I could have never established on my own.

Our secrets keep us ill and warped. I could not reject any findings from my inventory for they were the direct result of personal unmanageability and it was by my own design. There was nothing left to do but accept the fact that the best I could run my life got me exactly where I was at the time. It was a wonderful revelation because now I understood the matters I needed to work on and improve. I found that all I needed to change was my complete life!

I try to instill upon the minds of young people today that they need not fall to a bottom as I have known and the many years I abused myself. Instead, I try to explain to them how to raise that bottom to where they currently are and spare themselves years of agony. With some, the message gets through and unfortunately, with some it does not. We all have to go through whatever we must to find what is true and what is false. Meanwhile, I realize that every ounce of energy I put into helping, if it only changes one life, it has all been worth the complete giving of myself. Anything spoken from the heart is faith. It is our privilege to pass this along to others. We never know when we give of ourselves if we may possibly be saving the life of another. That is none of our business. What is important is the fact that we reached out with faith and made a great attempt. We do what we can do and God takes care of the rest. It is equally true that I have no idea what God's plans for someone else may be. Whatever the outcome may be for others and myself, I rest in faith knowing that the outcome is divine and well planned.

7 | Love

When my heart is with gratitude, I am in a state of completeness, having the ability to extend outgoing love and receive the love which is given unto me. Like the facets of a fine cut gemstone, it reflects light as it receives light. A diamond cannot be visible in the dark yet with a small amount of light it will begin to reflect its brilliance. We found the same analogy with our faith. Here is the fabric of our lives that determines our destiny and the purpose of our very existence. Love is not just a sensation; it is our complete demonstration of who we are and what we stand for. It is the whole balance of our life. God is love and love is God. Therefore, we cannot defy love itself. It would be resisting the natural laws, which cannot actually be broken. If you are in resistance of love in any form, you are only damaging yourself. Consider for a moment the fact that the greatest gift known to humankind was instilled into us and we set a course of corruption, self-seeking, dishonesty, betrayal and many other forms of contamination. Why would we possibly wish to damage the most magnificent gift of all? The conclusion is always the same. Self-seeking delivers the sharp blow of destruction. People may betray you but love itself will not.

I am grateful for the love I have known, experienced, received, and given. I retain the complete sum without reservation. It is much more important for me to love rather than to be loved. This is what keeps me balanced on the high wire of my own spiritual path. I have experienced betrayal and deep hurt of my own but I did not allow it to interfere with my faith in love. If anything, it has broadened my awareness of what love is, (and is not), and deepened my faith in the phenomenon of real love. As with any matter of the spiritual world, when we rise to our higher selves it allows us to give in a more pure form. It is here that we separate the wheat from the chaff. We also receive a great lesson and practice tolerance of others. We come to know the necessity to forgive the sins of others and ourselves because we are all too some degree emotionally ill.

In spousal or partner relationships, I have a little hesitancy with the term "falling in love". I do however believe with all that is in me that we grow in love. This is only my observation. Yours may be quite different. I do not wish to imply that the sensation of falling in love is not real, it certainly is. Time and experiences we share together are our greatest gifts and the fertile soil that two separate individuals grow together and towards. When we show kindness, compassion, and above all, the willingness to nurture the spiritual development of our significant other and our own, we are on the right path. We can bask in the sunlight of the spirit; all the time realizing this is a God given gift. I like to think of this as a time when our spirits come out and play beautifully together in harmony.

As with anything worthy and of real value, work is required to cultivate and nurture in order for it to blossom to potential. Love is neither obsessive nor possessive. It requires the freedom to stretch in its own capacity, which is truly beyond boundaries. Faith, trust, and honesty are imperative to the flow of its development. As humans, we are all fallible and we will make mistakes. Confusion may arise as we try to sort out the next right thing to do. People are fallible. God is not. Love is pure and we are all worthy. We cannot contaminate love; we contaminate ourselves. No matter how much we resist, truth will not allow its own destruction. Love itself does not stop because it is the presence and the whole of God. People enter our lives, we love them and sometimes they drift away but love itself remains the same. Today I am surrounded by love both incoming and outgoing, free from contamination or motives. Had I not made the mistakes I have, I doubt that I would possess the understanding and awareness I now carry at all times. My life is committed to try to carry a message of love, hope, and responsibility especially to young people that they do not have to make the same mistakes I made. They do not need to go through the years of self-torture that I put myself through and the beautiful result is, sometimes it works. This is not of my own personal power; it is the power of being a channel to give back what I have received. I do not have the ability to save a single soul but I can guide them to a path that they may walk with Love and find their own solutions. My reward is to see them begin to glow in the sunlight of the spirit. They are miracles happening before my eyes.

If you have never read the St. Francis Prayer, please do a little research and find it. Read it slowly and savor every word. This prayer contains the essence of love in its purest form and its practice returns gifts which are priceless. It is a recipe for love in honesty and completeness. Anyone who can honestly demonstrate the contents has truly risen to their higher selves. You will surely be one with your Creator. I fully believe that anytime we extend ourselves to another with love, we are raising ourselves to a mystical dimension. We hover above daily problems in living. I would state here that these *problems* are usually self-manifested and a matter of perception that we have the ability to change at any time. Again, God does not take anything away from me until I am ready to release it nor does He give me anything until I am ready to receive it. If this were not true, we would all be living and doomed to very stagnant and boring lives. There are those, too, who will go to great lengths to find reasons to justify actions they know within their soul to be wrong. It is unfortunate some will pursue false justification until death.

We are like the flowering plants that require pruning to reach their full blossom abilities. Sometimes we prune the branches that stretch to the sun and sometimes the roots from which it feeds. When we cut away the dead foliage, new growth appears. Is it not the same with love? When nurtured and cared for it becomes a masterpiece of beauty and fragrance to be visible and breathed in. What about the needy ones who will cross your path, that hunger for love and acceptance? Your answer to these simple questions is a picture of your own ability to demonstrate at the time. When we look within our heart, we can wash away the fragments of negativity from our soul. Once we walk past this crossroad, we never have to return to our old selves unless we choose to. That decision is entirely in your own hands. God will not interfere with the choices that you make. You are perfectly capable of picking your own misery and poisons or you can rise above, leaving the old behind you for the rest of your time and be a free spirit. You have the choice of fighting love or resting in your own passion for life. This is your decision and no one can make it for you.

My Creator has placed many people that have loved and helped me tremendously. Likewise, He has placed many people in my life that I would extend the same affection and care.

What an incredible experience this has been and continues to be. It is a never-ending circle of love new and fresh each day of my existence. It is in fact the greatest privilege I am granted. Anytime I am participating in this circle, I am not of God but I am with God. Over the years, I have found that it is here that I continually try to remain. It is a place of peace and beauty, which I nurture and protect yet there is no reason to defend my beliefs. In fact, within this realm, there is no room for my personal opinions. Whatever one believes is fine with me. I only know of my personal path and that which has and has not worked for me. Your entire life experience will most likely be different from mine but the important matter is that we are searching for a common solution for all of our problems. The answer is Love or God as they are the same.

Within the rooms of spiritual discussions I attend daily, I constantly see new faces and souls who are crying out. It is due to the defeat of living in self-will that drives them to a point of surrender. Though some of them arrive by judicial courts, many of them remain and seek change in their lifestyles. It is also true that some leave, returning to their past behaviors and die as a result. It is a sad fact. Their lives are consumed with pain, grief, anger, resentment, and a loss of all dignity. Then there are the *old timers* who have been upon a spiritual path for years that treat them with love and respect and offer them guidance to the solution for their every need. It is the restoration, or even at times, their first introduction to faith. For those who have looked at me for help, the first two things I try to help them overcome is anger and resentment, as these is, in fact, deadly subjects.

It is impossible to harbor resentments against someone unless the person means a great deal to you. Otherwise, it would not matter to begin with. Just what are resentments? It is when someone does us wrong once and we replay it repeatedly in our minds. It may be against humanity itself instead of another individual but we feel attacked. Are we not the ones who actually set the ball in motion because we had high expectations or we had placed someone upon a pedestal? That is a dangerous position to place anyone. What has happened to our ability to forgive the shortcomings of others and ourselves? Once we honestly consider these matters, they lose their power over us and begin to fall away. We find it foolish to squander away time and energy that may be beneficial to others in need of our service. We see that our prayers for others really work and it is constructive for all. Eventually we learn that love absolves all the combined negatives in our living and it becomes much easier to release the parts of ourselves that are questionable. Here again, we prune away that which stunts our growth.

To witness love in action is an incredible phenomenon. To extend or receive love without any conditions, expectations, or underlying motives is the true purpose of our being here on this earth. It is such a joy to see those around us begin the growth process and gain the ability to pass their findings along to others. To watch personal, positive changes develop is truly miraculous and very uplifting. I see those around me who once felt hopeless join life among the living, and witness some, perhaps for the very first time, participate in their own life. Smiles are on their faces replacing frowns from the pain of instability. Certainly, they fall down at times but to see them stand back up and resume the course is enlightening. This is the difference between human beings and human doings. My happiness for them is immeasurable and I stand in honor of their presence. They are seekers looking for more than they have known before. The paths that I speak of are the human soul in travel. The more truths and love we find, the more our soul cries out to sustain itself and to become further enriched in its magnificence.

We cannot define our Creator. Any attempt would be to place limitations upon Him. It is also true that God is Love; therefore we cannot accurately define love either. It has no limits or boundaries other than those we place upon it, yet humans do it all the time. Many times we see self-seeking motives confused or held in the name of love, when in fact love is not actually present. More often than not, we find it is actually lust for any number of objects. This has been the reason so many marriages fail. Perhaps there is an underlying thought of financial gain, physical attraction, power, co-dependency and the list goes on.

These matters have nothing to do with actual love. In fact, they destroy that which could become love. What I see most often is a lack of acceptance, or one partner tries to dominate the other's life. Someone in the arena tries to play God, which causes the relationship to be doomed. Any degree of equality is out the door. What most abusers fail to see is that they are really abusing themselves. They fail to see that when they go against the natural laws there is a hefty price to pay, just as in society's laws.

Bathe yourself in the sunlight of love that has no shame, guilt, regret, or remorse. It is here that you are truly with your Creator and He will smile upon you. My experience has been that I do not necessarily choose those that I would love; rather God puts people in my life and gives me the ability to love them all. I often think what a wonderful journey He has placed before me because it is the root system of living happy, joyous, and free. I know of no greater gift or anything more to wish. To me, this is the climax of living upon this plane and within this allotted time. I refuse to allow anyone or any circumstance to break my faith in love as I know it today, and tomorrow it will be even stronger. How do I *know* this? It is because I once lived a life of illusion, which was self-created and led to complete destruction. Each day that I dedicate to love strengthens the gate that opens up to me in whole. Love becomes a safe guard that keeps self-will out upon the battlefield away from the temple in which I live and dwell in spirit. My greatest enemy is always waiting just beyond this gate, ready to attack from all sides. I have respect for my enemy but I no longer carry fear because we have battled many times before. I lost many fights before I could claim victory and protect my territory. These are the wages of war between the heart and mind. There is no greater battle to fight and no greater victory to win. This is your freedom from bondage. It is also a battle of history that never has to repeat itself unless you choose to.

The happiness in our lives centers upon the love we allow. As with any other matter, the more we establish ourselves in love the more we receive. The more we give away the greater we are awarded. When we are growing in love, our consciousness continues to shift upward into a realm that is free from boundaries of development. Our Creator bestowed sexuality upon us to reproduce and to enjoy but this is only a tiny fragment of a very large picture. Practically everyone has abused their sexuality at some point and has hurt others and themselves. Some have used it as a weapon or for profit in different manners. This is simple abuse and has no impact on the power of love itself. Over a year ago I was in my second marriage when I underwent two lung surgeries. I discovered that my wife had been busy planning an affair with a former lover while I was going through the surgeries. At first, I was furious that she could do this at the time. After a couple of days, I looked into my heart and found forgiveness then I left and divorced her. I have no desire to see her again but love does not simply stop. I refuse to allow anyone or any matter to affect my personal love. I thought of the God given power of this ability and I soon thought Jesus loves me, yes He doo! This was a great revelation and resurrection. It was very clear to me that God was looking over my dominion. Although I felt a sting, love was completely unharmed. Jesus was also forsaken by one of His disciples, yet in His darkest hour, He offered prayer. Everything about His life was about proper demonstrations. Own and claim the spiritual growth you have achieved. At this point, you have claimed you are bad. Now comes the time to claim the good and wholesome.

8

Growth

Is it not a beautiful feeling to have your sails in the wind? The beautiful part about it is this. Just when we think life could not get much better, it does. Each new day presents opportunities to advance our awareness and understanding to greater levels. We find that we have undergone personality changes to meet and overcome the trials and tribulations in life. While the old life dissolves, a new life is evolving to take us places we could perhaps only dream. This is of course dependent upon our willingness to keep reaching out further every day. There have been times along my path that I felt I was not really going anywhere. It would feel as though I was stuck somewhere out in the universe. I have come to know that these are usually times when something much greater than I could fathom was about to reveal itself. It taught me to be careful and not be in a hurry; else I may miss something of great importance that I had not considered. I learned to have patience and wait for the revelation to appear without any force on my part. I continue to trust in that today. I am like the springtime bud of a plant that needs a little more sunshine and rain to flower. It happens right on time and under the right conditions.

Why would I choose to deceive myself by thinking I am any greater than the rose that blooms in the garden. We are all part of God's creations and they must all be connected and respected. We are never above His creations; we are merely a part of the flow. Our understanding and perceptions result in our awakening. This too is only the beginning of a far greater understanding, only in a blooming stage.

The greatest asset I am aware of concerning spiritual escalation is unity. As individuals, we can only know what we know. Sure, we have all had many personal experiences that have taught us well but as we extend and share our experiences with others, a completely different perception evolves. Piece by piece our lives become an open book, free of fear, judgments, and the secrets we have protected which kept us emotionally unstable. It is only by being together that we can become our whole selves and even societies for that matter. As I reflect back upon the events I have created, I see that many of them were hilarious and I wonder what I was thinking. Some of these events were painful but how would I know anything of equality and freedom had I not admitted and taken responsibility for my actions? We cannot grow beyond anything that we continue to lock inside and deny. I am certain that God has had a blast over some of the theories I have come up with as I looked for justification of my actions. The only justification is that we are human and bound to commit many ridiculous acts. The realization and awareness of that itself is a giant step toward individual and collective growth.

The greatest act of spiritual growth I know is to ask for help from God and others. It is when we are in this mindset that we are admitting we do not have the answers. It is also a great tool for ego deflation. Our egos tell us we should know the answers to our problems. When something wonderful happens in our life the ego says hey, look what I have done instead of giving credit to our Creator, which is the source of our gift. Likewise, when something terrible happens our ego says, look what I have caused, which brings shame, guilt, and remorse. My wife of twenty-eight years had a massive stroke when she was thirty-one and I honestly believed it was my fault. I walked around for years hating myself. I do not possess such powers. Our egos have to be demolished if we are to grow much at all. Our experiences in life simply happen and that which does not kill us makes us strong when we face it. However, we are not expected to face these matters alone. Again, we turn to unity with God and our fellows that a healing process begins. If this were not true, creation would have stopped with Adam and Eve. Our purpose here is to love, respect and help one another and we should do so with gratitude and honor. What are we really but trusted servants? Consider the power in that itself.

The lifetime partner of growth is change. We are never going to know the complete truths in this life. Only God knows that and He is the One who never changes. Completeness cannot change or even be described. As we inventoried our lives as honestly as possible we found many matters that were not desirable. The shortcomings we find are not simply eliminated from us and that is a wonderful acknowledgement. Instead, we see a lifelong process that requires willingness and great challenges ahead for all remaining time. When I first truly faced myself, I was overwhelmed at all the changes I needed to make and, honestly, I felt discouraged. I did not realize that time is our greatest friend and healer. I sat out on a course to find a set of principles to live by. It took several years to conceive how deep rooted my defects were engrained but, meanwhile, I had begun the necessary work to change what I could at the time. The more I practiced these principles, the more my conscious level began to shift. The result was I became more serene and my fears slowly began to vanish. I felt that I was in proper hands. To present date I am aware that personal defeat is victory over long term battles.

I love this stuff; and really that is all that it is. It is just stuff. I change my focus and awareness from what I can or cannot do to what our Creator and we can accomplish together. Upon each awakening, we find new challenges to meet and the opportunity to practice our principles. As we do this day by day, we also see that our principles grow to even greater meaning and purpose themselves. We search for ways to expand them with better understanding and to find new principles that are yet to be revealed. We have a hunger that is not entirely fulfilled. Like the rosebush, when one of the flowers wilt we remove it from the bush and several more are born. It is the same principle when we give of ourselves to others. Our experience, strength, and hope are given to others in need and they bloom in beauty. It is a spirit of rotation that is never ending and without bounds. It is the same experience as the four seasons. The old dies out and the new is reborn. This is true with all creation. In the fall of the year, the leaves of our trees turn beautiful colors and fall away. The sap of the tree returns to its roots, which expand and grow deeper resulting in a stronger foundation. The tree itself continues to grow and become larger. In the spring, we see new branches and new growth. Your life is no different at all. With the passion of spiritual growth, we become the trees that will support new life. Birds will nest and reproduce within the branches as earth renews itself from the cold and dark days of winter to the warmth and sunshine of spring.

Our will for life among the living is entirely up to us as individuals. Will is a very important word to me as I borrowed from others at a time when I had only very little. I lived in the southwest United States for some years and if you have ever been around the Grand Canyon you can see pinion trees that are hundreds of year's old, living in complete rock. The Saguaro cactus lives in the desert sand, dust and rock and it takes seventy-five years, (I am told), to produce its first arm. I have lived in Alaska and witnessed daylight re-appear and the snows melt. The grass has been turning green underneath before the snow has melted. Mother Nature herself teaches us will and strives for survival and development. The time is today that we should be living within the natural laws and order of the universe. If someone should ask me how to live a spiritual life I would answer, do it today. This is as simple as it gets and the only complexities are those we choose to create. What I choose will either make or break me and I have gratitude for my brokenness.

My Creator has clearly done for me what I could not do for myself, and equally He does not do for me what I can do for myself. He does not make my decisions nor does He create my outlook upon life. These are entirely my choices. I will either rejoice, or suffer the consequential outcome of my decisions. Believe me; I get gentle reminders if I drift back into self-will. My mistakes only instruct me to get back on the path and conjure up another springtime day. Anytime this occurs in my life I find the same solution: get out of me, get with God and try to help someone else. It always takes me right back to where I need to be, without fail. As our conscious level has risen, we find this is the only solution and always the next right thing to do. We realize the value of sharing that which we have and have not. This is simple clarity in growth. "I do not have, but I need from you" should always be taken for strength instead of weakness. This is the survival skill needed for your family tree to grow upon the rocks, and grow it shall.

For the efforts we have made we are rewarded greater awareness, awakenings, and at times, spiritual experiences. We
are aware such changes are far beyond that which we could
have accomplished alone. Often, others see our transforma-
tions before we do. We come to see, feel, and believe we are
guided toward a much more purposeful state of being. I never
know what, how, or where that will lead me and it is actually
none of my business or concern. What is important to me is
that I continue the search on a daily basis. Deep inside of me
is a feeling of being homesick for some place I have yet to go
and somehow this feeling remains alive and protected by a
power I will never fully understand. My job is to respect, accept, and protect it to the best of my ability and to give away
any gains to others in a free and loving manner. Any gains I
have made upon this life have been a direct result of losing
the life I had created in my mind, body, spirit, and actions. My
medication was the experience, strength, and hope of others
that had lived as I had lived and died as I have died and our
paths somehow connected on this earth. This experience is no
different from the old pinion trees of the high cliffs in Arizona
or the cactus of the low desert that survives, more or less,
upon will. Is God not breathing life into us so our eyes and
hearts may see the beauty of life growing from nothing?

Do we have memories of any time in our life that complete
defeat, pain and anguish fell upon us? Have we thanked God
that they are only memories no matter how painful? It means
we have survived and lived another day. Have we been capable of reaching out to someone else without advice, opinion,
or any self-seeking motives whatsoever and acknowledged
we are there for their support? If you can acknowledge that
you honestly have been in that position and delivered, you
have truly served your purpose for this day. That in itself is
perhaps all you need to know about spirituality. This is not a

religion; it is a way of life that supports the life of others. The good we demonstrate today is the building blocks for our tomorrows. As we continue to see areas we can make positive changes and take responsibility for and have earnest willingness to face anything that may entail, we will find ourselves standing in the essence of growth. Our sails collect the wind and keep us on a moving course to distant shores we have longed to see and walk on. Our days and nights at sea may have been stormy at times but we are now standing on solid ground. It is a wonderful opportunity to make many new discoveries in a new place.

9

Acceptance

Here is the solution to all of our problems, great and small. In the early years of my journey, I desperately looked for honest answers to what had been a sea of lies of my existence. I will never have the answers but after a good deal of time, the questions began to melt away and seem no longer very important. As I place my will and life into my Creator's hands each day, my very life is really none of my business. My duty is to show up, participate and trust. Events happen in life that I have no idea where they come from or where they will take me. All I know is that they are only experiences and they all teach me in one way or another. They may be unpleasant or joyous. Whichever the case may be, I seldom have any power over them. If there is a matter I can change for the better, I am willing and begin the necessary work to correct the circumstance. Otherwise, I can only accept the matter and rest in thought that it has its reason. After years of practice, I noticed a remarkable discovery. As my rejections became less my acceptance would grow to new heights. This may be common knowledge for some folks. For me a new light came on. It became clear there was less that I needed to battle, giving me more time and energy to be of help to others. It involved acquiring more faith because in all honesty I cannot judge whether the experiences that occur in my life are good or bad. I can only trust that if it crosses my path it usually has significant reason. The key question I ask myself in any given situation is: "Was it I who created the situation?" If that is true then I am the one who has to change it.

I cannot reject any negatives in my life until I first accept that they are there. Matters arrive which occupy some thread of my life that I feel is undesirable. By my own admission, I have to ask myself if this is something I can change or do I need to place it entirely in God's hands. Surprisingly, I find that many times I am quite capable of making adjustments because I utilize a degree of power and courage from The Source. We have consciousness, heart, and soul for a reason. I do not suffer the illusion that I simply dump my life on my Creator. Cleaning matters up when I am capable is my responsibility. We can smile as we go through our daily task of being present and growing in unity and humility. What purpose would I have in growth if I cannot pass it along to others? I require the help of others in my life. I cannot live completely alone. If I cannot accept others exactly, where they are, what they have to offer, would there be a need for human companionship? The crossing of our paths in life is not coincidental. We may not see it at the time but it has an intended purpose. You may have something I need or I may have something you need. The point is we need one another and this can hardly evolve unless there is first acceptance. Likewise, we do not grow in strength until we accept our weaknesses.

Life need not be a struggle. If we stay on the course, we eventually find ourselves in a position and mentality that we cease to fight anyone or anything in the manner we once have known. This does not mean we allow any type of abuse what-soever. We have every right and obligation to rid ourselves of any abusive conditions. Whenever we meet someone who is experiencing such a dilemma it is our duty to help them rise above it and find safety and sanctuary. Counselors see women show up with fresh bruises. Teachers see a child on the play-ground over in some corner alone with its head held down. Clergy hear horrid confessions from those who feel there is no other place to turn. Consider the police who react to domestic disturbances every day. These victims, consumed by fear and rejection, live in dark places where we must bring light. These are healthy battles and victory over them must be won. We may have to accept such matters in the scene of admission itself but we clearly do not accept such behaviors to continue. In my first book, "Dissolve into Evolving", I spoke of the seven deadly sins, and later I read that there are actually only two sins and they are abusing the spiritual development of others or our own spiritual development. Both are true and very real. Any time you see the threat against one's spiritual growth you will certainly find the seven deadly sins violated. We have to keep in mind that we are not God but we are trusted servants always willing to lend a helping hand where and when pos-sible.

We come to see acceptance cannot be an all or nothing at-titude. The only thing in my life that is all or nothing is God and my faith. Circumstances arise, changes occur, and new problems may arrive. No matter what the situation we need ask only two questions. Can I change it or do I need to accept it and place the outcome in His hands. We use our courage to change that which we can and rest in serenity when we place matters in The Wise One's hand. I have only two options, where my Creator has countless possibilities. I do well to stand out of the way and witness the performance of miracles as they come to be. Every single day I see new people show up in the rooms of spiritual discussions who are at battle with their own selves and accepting their situation, I see those who have been around a short time who are developing their own root system and those who have been involved for many years that help to guide. What an amazing process this truly is. The old easily accepts the new for they have lived in the darkness themselves and have clear knowledge of the pain. The new accepts the old because they hear of experience, strength, and hope and it is the serenity the young ones long to witness. We breathe life into the dead. We give hope to the hopeless. We direct them to a path they must walk themselves but we continue to guide them at times. It is here that we realize the power of acceptance of others because we are, in fact at the time, part of the process of life rejuvenating itself. The horrors of life come to close and the new is born, all stemming from acceptance that always leads us to faith and hope, the very fabric of dependence. This determines the future happiness of our existence.

Each day in meditation requires me to accept who I am, what I am, and where I am and acknowledge this to my Father. Within this process, I am free and feel the sense that I am in protective custody of The Source. How could I love and demonstrate gratitude for my freedom had I not once been self-incarcerated? How could I reach out to others with unconditional love had I not felt unlovable? Why would I seek out the truths in life had I not lived in an ocean of lies? We desire to freely give others that which we once felt denied because we wish for them better living. These are but a few of the responsibilities we assume as a direct result of self-acceptance. We do not wait for the next batter to step up to the plate maybe scoring a run. Our goal is to knock the ball out of the park so everyone gets to go home. We take this attitude because it has become our duty and a way of life that works where the old one had failed.

Our self-sufficiency has to be abandoned and reliance upon some form of Higher Power be considered if we are to have any prospect of spiritual growth. It is that simple and factual. Otherwise, we continue doing the same as we have always done, expecting different results. You may certainly expect different results as life will become more miserable and prove that to you each day. Our negative thoughts, actions and re-actions are just as powerful as the positive. Here again, you have a simple choice to make and I pray God be with you in your decision, as He does not demand your participation.

10

Into the Mystic

Every particle of my life today involves the affirmation of that which I have found and that I have yet to acknowledge. It is not, however, a place to lodge and rest but rather a pathway to continue moving. I truly love the awareness of spirits in motion and I am very happy being a part of the flow. When I lived in Alaska, I witnessed the spawning of salmon, which lay their eggs and pounded themselves against the currents until death in order for life to resume. Often they would be a meal for the bears to sustain their lives or drift into the current to supply other needs. I clearly recall walking upon the banks of rivers there and along the Colorado River in the southwest examining the beautifully colored pebbles that had once been large rocks and the current of these rivers shaped and polished these beautiful stones. Time cannot be answered it can only be observed and accepted. It carries a song inside of us all, which is more of a prayer to continue to be a part of a current where life supports life and death is a part of rejuvenation.

The practice of solid principles allows us to become mediums in the spiritual world where we witness the magical and supernatural. Life flows through us. We hold the truths that we find and the negatives we let go of, to determine our boundlessness, or disconnection from gravity, as we have known it. There is always that thirst to reach that which we do not know or understand. We are seekers and if we seek, we shall find. Whether we turn to the Shaman, the Sorcerer, or the Spiritualist, we occupy a place where we must find our own answers. The only blueprint to life is that which we have drawn and how we have chosen to animate our existence. Many people hear the words mystical or supernatural and think it to be practically impossible to perceive and far away from reach. Our minds tell us we should settle for what we have and be content to remain, while our souls cry out for something more. I do not reside in my mind alone because this is where my restrictions exist, breeds, and tells me I must abide by made up rules. This is a false notion. If God or whatever you choose to call Him were truly our Father, why would we possibly think we are not free to dwell in His house? Some understand this as heaven, where they wish to go after they die. I certainly do not wish to interfere with anyone's beliefs for that is your path and I am on mine. Our perceptions may differ as we seek the same destination.

I do not know exactly when it happened but after considerable effort, my faith was born. I discovered I could rise above the walls I had constructed and become a free being. I do not believe we are simply here in a game of survival without much more purpose or reason. When I turned over my will and life there was an open invitation developed, where God and I inhabit the same breath of air and we reside inside each other. As we were created, so do we have the ability to create with absolute freedom of choice? If you choose borders, self-incarceration, strife, or suffering that is exactly what you shall have. The day you decide to abandoned self-will and make a conscious decision to live in free will, so you will know the magic of existing in a very different realm. How do we define the supernatural or mystical other than the awareness of walking beside and inside our Creator? We need not wait for that which is currently present in the very moment. If you are waiting for anything more significant to occur in life, you will continue waiting. Chances are you have received many invitations already. Do not continue to be the child alone on the playground because their life is abused and severely compromised, the battered wife who wonders if she will be beaten or abused tonight. Every domestic disturbance call to law enforcement is a direct result of one person's need to be right and attempt to prove the other wrong. This very concept divides many families each day. Consider for a moment how ridiculous this is and the price attached to such behavior. Claim your lack of understanding. Claim what belongs to you good and bad, make your corrections, then go out into life and have a blast. Allow your actions to demonstrate that there is nothing to defend or proclaim. If I am truly seeking God's will, I find no reason for either of the two. I do not invade the territory of others nor do I commiserate. I extend a hand to those who do not understand how to begin their journey, and support their efforts along the way.

Our spiritual awareness or perhaps our first experiences are only the very beginning of a newfound way of life. As long as we retain willingness and effort, we see the possibility of unlimited development, as long as we understand that we have no possession of our prized gifts. Any individual's spiritual assets, are better shared that we may all live in a better place where freedom of spiritual travel is allotted to every soul without any thought of monopoly of them. In fact, our true happiness is a result of how much we can give ourselves away without any expectations of gratuities for the labor of our efforts. However, we are greatly awarded simply by being present in a system of life that supports our new life. The death of an old way of living is resurrected by the new and unbound. Matters that were once taken for granted or unappreciated are awakened, imbued with greater depth and clarity. Our complete attitude, outlook, and perception changes in ways we can never fully explain. There is no explanation needed as we are perfectly comfortable to witness and experience our moments in time. It is important to realize that these very moments are especially for you. We are in fact standing in the presence of our Creator in real time that, seemingly, appears out of nowhere. Messages appear to us that we have never considered, bringing about even more awareness and greater sensitivity.

Spiritual prosperity comes to all who seek and allow it. The Divine is always there and the only matter that ever blocks us is our self-will and warped motives. In my fifty-eight years of life, God has not once imposed upon me but He has always been there when I was ready to receive. When I reflect back upon the beginning of my journey, it seemed to come slowly. I did not consider for a long time the fact that I was growing out of one life and growing into another. Of course this took time as I had much to unlearn and much more to consider. The truths of life have existed since the creation of man. Actually, it did not require my searching, but rather my acceptance. What I did not understand for a long period was the fact that all of my changes would happen in His time and not mine. I had to be, quite simply, habilitated.

Today, life is not waiting on spiritual experiences rather life is a spiritual experience. It always has been. I just did not understand or consider that fact. I am not here to endure. I am here to stand in amazement as my remaining life unfolds. I live in a complete separate reality from what I had once lived. I found and walked the path towards home. I would have never thought of the treasures which would arrive from the simple admission of complete defeat. Is the mystical anything more than standing with your entire life before our Creator looking in the moment and laughing over the foolishness of the past? This is the dividing line between mere existence and a connected life. The great question is what will we choose? I have made a decision and rest in serenity and comfort of what has proven to be a much better way. Any plans for all my tomorrows have been prearranged. When I awake each day they will appear. It is in my best interest that I simply follow. I do not have the sum of all equations that will arrive in my life. That is God's business and not mine. My understanding is not nearly as important as my quest to understand. We seek out for one single reason; we wish to know and expand our personal relationship with The Great Mystery in which we place all trust and connectivity from past, present, and future, should we be granted a tomorrow.

As we connect to this amazing consciousness, our life transforms far beyond any powers that we could create alone. We have changed. For all practical reasons, we have stepped outside of ourselves, from what we have previously believed and into a completely different realm. People who have known us usually see the change long before the individual in transformation becomes aware of what is taking place. What they often do not see is the fact that we are changing together. Their own perception changes and allows them to grow in trust and faith, adding a little more light and love into life. In my earlier days upon my path I had sudden experiences that seemed to be earth- shaking. Although those times were very significant, the most important things of which I am aware happened over a great deal of time and required much effort, honesty, and willingness. I became far more interested in the lives of others than of my own. I did not plan this rather it was a time of my first steps to grow from a selfish life into becoming selfless. I was cared for even though I did not sense it at the time. I have no more idea today where my personal journey will lead me than from my very first day of surrender. I do not wish to know or consider any outcomes. In all reasoning, I am just along for the ride to whatever destination I am to visit. I do not have the first clue of what that may entail.

I find comfort living the journey I am upon today. I have been and will remain for the rest of my days a pupil of spiritual living. Although I freely share what I have received so far, I am not a teacher. I am merely a friend to others and a channel, to be utilized however God sees fit. Living within this realm is the greatest definition of the mystical I know of. It is not so much about sudden shifts as it is about time itself, well spent in patience, tolerance, honor, and above all, unconditional love, which we have a capacity to freely share at any given moment. All strong foundations materialize from this cornerstone and the words, the thoughts, and the actions, transcend onto those who seek. We are happy to give the good in ourselves to others expecting nothing in return. We have found the more we invest in others the greater our own character strengthens. As this process continues, are we not outside of ourselves and within a far greater power? If we were not demonstrating from love would we have any regard for the welfare of others? Spiritual reality occurs when our minds are out of the clouds and we walk upon this earth where our fellow travelers dwell and are likewise seeking. This is not spiritual make believe, it is reality projected by The Great Mystic. Our hearts, souls, and minds are free to travel anywhere in the cosmos but gravity holds our feet on the ground.

Whether you are just beginning a spiritual journey or have been walking your path for years, allow yourself to be completely fearless and as completely honest as possible. As you look into yourself, have no fear of what you find. When I consider this, I remind myself that my life is a completely borrowed experience. Nothing belongs to me and yet I belong to so much. This being said I have nothing to fear and no more dark rooms to hide my character flaws. If we did not possess these shortcomings what purpose or desire would there be to seek changes from the deepest areas of our souls? Enjoy your life, as it is truly mystical and supernatural. Your changes will always arrive right on time. Each of your experiences have meaning though the understanding of them may come far later on. Embrace your moments with the understanding that God chooses you to be alive today. This choice could have been different.

11

Happiness

Every day I see newcomers stagger into the rooms looking for solutions and another way of living, and my heart becomes filled with joy and happiness. I clearly recall my earliest days filled with amazement of new discoveries, pain of the past, and directed to a source that would bring great relief from what I thought was a hopeless life. To witness others make this transition is true joy. The happiness I have today is a direct result of faith in my Creator and those who gave of themselves, helping me find the way out of my own seclusion. There was great hope given to me that I would later pass along to others, feeding a system that remains self-supporting. Anything I am capable of giving away today is a result of what I received in my yesterdays. Again, I do not possess this. I can only be a servant or messenger of that beyond possession, and filled with gratitude. Happiness always travels forward giving to all who is in its path. Whether I am sharing with another individual or a group, I get to see eyes light up as they step from dark into light in wonder and amazement. It may take a little time but we see them awaken to a world of new possibilities that contain great adventures. They begin to collect a set of spiritual tools that will sustain themselves under any conditions if used wisely.

My happiness today is in proportion to my freedom from bondage of a life lived upon self-will. I do not have problems today rather I have challenges at times to meet and overcome. This is how I earn my faith and courage. I face what is in front of me with a degree of joy from realizing something else I need to turn my attention and work. What I once dreaded I now look forward to as a new opportunity to expand myself. This allows me to witness even more miracles than known before. Daily self-inventories allow us to see where we are, what work needs to be done, and the promise of a better tomorrow. The only time I delve in self is strictly for the sake of examination. How can I be of greater service, what can I freely give to another, and most important, how can I better serve my Creator? What goodness do I have to contribute to society? These are questions I look at each day allowing me to remain aware of a purpose for being. In reality, this life is about ninety-five percent of how I take it and about five percent of how I make it. In short, we should not take ourselves too seriously. When I share with a new person today, I can laughingly express some of the really stupid things I have done. This accomplishes a couple of different things; they realize that matters of their own past no longer needs to be top secret and it establishes an element of trust which they probably have not known in a long time. They come to understand that we laugh together as opposed to laughing at someone.

The greatest prescription for happiness I know of is continuing to move forward in our work of maintaining spiritual freedom and emotional balance. Here, again, is the great importance of living in the moment. The minute we start projecting outcomes, worry and fear, guilt and pride, we are severely jeopardizing serenity. If we find ourselves doing these things, we should stop and take a few deep breaths and acknowledge that we are actually allowing negativity in our consciousness. Negative thoughts can dominate us very quickly but we always have the choice to accept or reject, and the choosing of one or the other dictates our moods. These thoughts are no more or no less than our imagination. Mood changes are just as natural as breathing. They are perfectly normal. To me this is the calling out for a spot check of my personal inventory. The majority of time I see that I am out of alignment. I have automatically jumped to a conclusion before thinking something through and given it proper consideration. We are going to experience and feel every mood known. This is necessary but we do have the ability to make adjustments anywhere or anytime as needed. We are created to be happy joyous, and free. Consider for a moment that this is your very purpose of existence. Do not merely expect happiness; demand it, for it is your gift created especially for you. No matter how deeply you care for others, you are the only person that can exist in your own skin. Your body and mind is your temple, your house, your complete experience. When you have cleaned it to the point it sparkles, and tossed out all the clutter of unused or damaged items, when you have placed windows in every room to allow sunlight, your house will be in order. Your remaining time will require keeping it that way. Every day of existence should include cleaning the cobwebs from the mind that may deflect rays of the true sunlight.

As humans, we have a great tendency to become complacent. Often we may think that life is wonderful just the way it is. I have come to know over the years that complacency can easily become the beginning of deterioration. Our day may be completely grand and we have much gratitude to relish. The danger comes when we find ourselves at rest and no longer seeking more understanding and improvement. Spirituality requires continuing to move forward in healthy achievements. It was only after admitting my weaknesses and realizing how dependent I was upon my Creator and the help of others that I would know humility. This was the backbone of achieving true freedom and happiness. The better I understand this, the more my need becomes. Years ago, I thought the measure of man was his independence, when in fact it is the complete opposite. Perhaps one day, humans of all nations will come to realize that whoever lays down the weapons of self-destruction first will be the winner. The only war ever needed to be fought is the battle against individual inner turmoil. History has clearly shown that entire civilizations have been lost needlessly, yet this turmoil seems to continue more than ever. Through my own eyes, I see a race of who can abuse the seven deadly sins to the most extremes. In the same vision, I see these sins continue to be ignored, and attempts to cover the problems up, all due to complacency.

The great problem that exists and the root cause of all unhappiness is the fact that humankind with all the technical advancements and knowledge we have acquired, we have yet to learn how to love one another and share our resources and fulfill our needs. The arc of light that we put out individually is contagious. It brings hope to the insanity we witness each day. When we turn on the news each day we see citizens of different nations uprising and attempting to overthrow their government systems because they are poison, and keep them hungry, diseased, homeless, and hopeless in practically every area of their lives. As difficult as this is to conceive and try to understand the chaos, these people are rejecting the old systems which have not worked. They are seeking a better way. The path to peace, harmony and love cries out from those denied their true purpose.

Even though these outer problems are a part of what appears to be reality today, we should and must retain our individual happiness, love, and freedom. Neither you nor I have the power to change the world but eventually we begin to change our world. We continue individually and collectively to shine a light of attraction that others will see and begin to follow. Perhaps the rebellion we see in the world today will be positive. Perhaps the resurrection of humankind is arriving and change is near. Whatever the outcome I choose to continue my personal journey, however these thoughts shine a different light on the term "weapons of mass destruction". I believe we have all felt the impact of this horrible bomb far too long and reaching far too wide. When I compare my own life to the shortcomings I see today, I have to acknowledge that a good deal of my personal life suffered the same defiance. What would I know and how much gratitude would I have today of love, serenity, and freedom had I not known and lived in the opposite? I see the magnificence of God's creations in nature and looking into the sky at night, I consider all the wonder and beauty that is visible to any human being. Yet I felt I had to hide that which I created myself. I later discovered that creation cannot be hidden, especially that of my own.

I walked into a room today where a mirror was hung upon one of the walls and attached underneath it was a sign that read, "You are looking at the problem". I began to think of many years before when I learned "if I am not the problem there is no solution". Even years later, I have come to know that I am not a problem rather I am a process in motion. Today I live in progress never seeking perfection. The human mind can easily dictate our lives. If I think I am a problem that is exactly what I will be. If I believe I am a part of a solution, there I will exist. No one, no government, organization, or any institution can take this away unless I allow it to happen. I think I can safely say that this very matter is a great part, reason, and essence of my own journey. I happily continue toward the light where the truths I may come to know lay waiting in time.

I do not consider myself a religious man. I sincerely feel my purpose is among the spiritual and there are many of whom have great knowledge of the religions. I love to read the Psalms from the Bible. These are individuals speaking to God at their own level asking for guidance and understanding, and offering praise. One of my favorites is the one hundred forty-forth psalm, in which man asks the question;" what is man that you would care for him"? As I stare into the clear night-time sky and see His creations that are light-years away and realize how small I really am, what is God that He cares for me? As I continue the trail of self-searching in humility, the answers come to some of my deepest questions as I become fit and aware to receive them. The walk itself has become the answer to all my personal questions and problems for that matter. The more my awareness develops the more my questions and problems dissolve. This leaves me in a neutral state that presents an open channel for my Creator to guide my daily living, including what I think and how I feel. In this, alone, I find great joy, happiness, and peace within my place in this universe. I am no longer attempting to live faster than my angels can fly.

There are messages, sometimes temporarily hidden, in every experience of our lives. Every single moment has meaning whether we realize this or not. If we turn back to the one hundred and forty- second and one hundred and forty- third Psalms, and especially verse three, we can clearly see that we are our own greatest enemy. It is only after a great dose of the inner truth and with much needed humility that we begin to ascend from the great storm and realize that it was only by the grace of God that we survived. A very clear definition of man's darkness is revealed and yet we find ourselves as lambs that arrive to The Father as we pass through these windows of change. Complacency has no place in our lives. We are well aware that a storm can always become more severe and we can descend into still deeper darkness. We cannot afford to fool ourselves about this. Armed with consciousness the only sensible option is to continue forward in our work towards freedom from bondage of self. The dividends of our effort will prevail as we patiently find ourselves without expectations and continue seeking to do the next right thing. The revelations of The Father may seem slow but they are *always* right on time. We come to realize that patience and tolerance of others and ourselves is a precious virtue to cherish. There is no point trying to rush our lives and the experiences we will encounter. By doing so, we are gambling with our own happiness.

Anytime I find myself attempting to run the *show of life* again, I have to stop and realize that there is a great chance I am interfering with divine intervention. I am trying to get the universe to align with me instead of aligning myself to the universe. History has proven this never works very well for me. In fact, it is sneaking up on being a terroristic threat! The happiness I hold today is a byproduct of getting out of me and getting into you. Any time the opportunity to give away everything good I have learned from my deepest struggles and see a face light up with new hope pleases me beyond words. As a recovering alcoholic and addict that I truly am and having gone through the lowest bottoms known to man, I am happy to take the hand of men and women who cross my path who are seeking liberation from an unending disease of spiritual and emotional illness. To see their eyes begin to shine, smiles come to their faces and embark on a life that is fresh and new is amazing. These are people from all occupations, rich and poor, knowledgeable, and without a clue, but we share a commonality. The desire to become better is more valuable than any vein of gold we could possibly strike. We can only live in this state if we are willing to give all the dividends away as we received them. They are *all* God given and intended to share.

We should happily rejoice with others and ourselves because we have experienced much and traveled far. Along our path, we have clearly witnessed how our own experience, strength, and hope aided others who are seeking. To reflect past miseries and laugh about most of them today is paramount. We have truly risen above the gloom practically all of us have known. We have a much broader understanding of reason and it allows us to flow more freely in our passions. Passion, like intellect, has little purpose unless we live it, feel it, and it flows through us just like the blood in our veins. Joy is contagious! As we demonstrate our freedom and happiness, it attracts others who give it to still others, and a chain reaction takes place. Each day that I attend twelve-step meetings, I always hear something new to consider and help me along my path. The sense of unconditional love and caring for each other fills the air like an electrical charge that is seen and heartfelt. We accomplish what none of us can do alone. No one of us will ever have all the answers. We are simply sharing a wonderful journey I believe pleases God and Christ very much. What greater happiness could we ever know or hope to know?

For all the wonderful gifts and blessings I have known, there is not a single reason to congratulate myself. They are all byproducts of seeking His will for my existence. When I first began my recovery from alcoholism and drug addiction, happiness was not my goal. In fact, it seemed so far away that I could not perceive it at the time. I was very fortunate and grateful that the obsession was entirely removed but I did not have a clue how to live well. It was only after I cleaned up the wreckage of my past, which turned out to be a complete overhaul, that I began to experience and get my first glimpses of freedom and true happiness. My greatest comfort came years later when I understood that I am not the god of my past nor am I the god of my future. My entire living, dying, and re-birth experience happened exactly as it was intended. I arrived right on time. One day more out there may have physically killed me and one day less and I may not have been entirely ready to face complete defeat. Though I did not realize it at the time, God had always been there looking over me. He had never left me. I had left Him. What was perfectly clear was that I lived as I had lived and died as I should die. There was nothing to argue. This was a pathway; I had to claim responsibility for my past for any future growth to take place.

12| Humility

Spiritual blindness falls upon everyone at some point and time. If this were not true, man would not cry out his shortage. The word itself is often mistaken for humiliation, which is in fact an opposite of humility. This is the arena and the time that we step outside of our darkness and into a new light that brings great hope to our souls. It shines a light, however dim, to that which was once written off as a lost cause. It is cause for continuation of that which we do not fully understand or have severely abused. The antidote is very simple. All we have to do is ask and a new reality is born. It does not matter who you are, what religion, creed, race, or any other possible questions one may have, it is readily available to all that breathe in air of the spirit. Though my own experience and yours may be quite different, I found that the greater the misery developed by living in self-will the more willingness to change came to be. The first truth I had to swallow about myself when I first arrived at a treatment center was the very best I knew how to live my life had gotten me exactly where I was and needed to be. Again, I believe this was divine intervention.

Everything concerning my life today that is good and whole-some is a daily gift. I do not possess anything really. If I take care, respect and nurture these gifts on a daily basis there is a good chance I will know them tomorrow. Every human has a dark side. We have intellect, which is compatible with humil-ity as long as we place humility first. I can have great spiritual knowledge but it is worthless unless I utilize and practice it in all my affairs. I continue to be amazed every day that I speak with my Creator and acknowledge my weaknesses, strength is given to me. What a truly amazing process this actually is. Before each A.A. meeting I attend daily I ask God to get *me* out of the way and allow me to be a channel of His love, care, and His will. When I share with others my weaknesses are ap-parent because I claim them, therefore I am not speaking in terms of personal power but rather sharing how I have been blessed and my personal struggles. I consider my thoughts and words that they may be helpful to another being. In doing so, I am not a message I am only taking others to the mes-sage itself. I do not have anyone's answers. The most I can possibly do for another is walk with them as they begin their journey to the point they are upon solid ground. In Alcohol-ics Anonymous, we call this sponsorship. My greatest prayer that I ask for each of those I take under wing is that they will outgrow me and fire me to find someone who better suits their needs and future development. I praise these times that I have known before and my hope is the pattern will never be broken. It is perfect in its entirety.

Humility is my pathway to faith. It begins each morning in meditation as I look at who I am, what I am and where I am and take responsibility of what I find. I think one of the greater questions I ask myself is; what is my vision of life? As I have self-searched, what is it that I see? Considering my entire life so far, good and bad, it has been one long party filled with joy and pain, gladly accepting it all today. I think of all the beautiful people God has chosen for our paths to meet, the wonderful events gifted, and the amazing fellowship which surrounds me with brothers and sisters, that we are all equals. The second question I ask is; how can I become better and give more? The answers reveal themselves practically each day if I am in proper alignment. This *alignment* however is completely my own responsibility. There are no quick fixes. It has taken me years of effort and a great deal of outside help to arrive at the spiritual peace I feel today. After all this time, I realize I know very little. I have only scratched a surface of endless possibilities. All accomplishments in my life are a result of God working through me and it is He to whom I give all credit. In present day, I still fumble accepting compliments and I believe it is due to the awareness that it is not about me at all. I have recently learned to reply, thank you for your awareness that God is working in my life. To take personal credit is very far from the actual truth of my being.

Maybe all I really know of humility is that over the years I have digested some large portions of humble pie. That is as it should be. I cannot nor do I wish to reverse my experiences in life. There is a saying that nothing goes wasted in God's economy. How true this really is. The years I was an active alcoholic and addict, I would experience the awful pain, guilt, shame, fear, and remorse, I had no vision other than I was going to die of addiction. I had no comprehension that perhaps I would one day help others recover from the vicious cycle. I am not a teacher, but as I become an instrument, I try to carry the message that no one has to go through what I did for so long. Those days were *my experience* at that time. *My strength* arrived from complete defeat. *My hope* is that I continue to be a channel that God works through to help another being if only in a very small way. After all, I remember that it was only by grace that I survived. Though I try to treat everyone equally, I must confess that I have a particular soft spot for the young people I see coming through the doors of A.A. I think of how wonderful it is to have hit a spiritual bottom at such a young age and watch their eyes begin to brighten as they realize they are no longer alone. I think about the beauty of discovery that is before them and the fact that they do not have to suffer the insanity anywhere near as long as many of us have. Their home lives may have been less than desirable, but within the spirit of the fellowship, they may find parent figures, grandparents, and brother and sister relationships that sustain them very well. They do not normally realize it at the time but as they begin to share about their battles, they are taking their very first steps toward humility. They soon learn they do not have to be subjects of humiliation, real or imagined, any longer.

As we realize exactly what our character defects are by cleaning up the wreckage of the past, we ask God to remove them from us. It is important to realize that it took a great deal of time to become as warped as we are, so naturally it is going to take time, prayer, work, and patience to live ourselves out of our flaws. I remember feeling a deep void within me. It was a process I had to work through to allow God's love and service to others is present in my life. During this time to present, I would receive lessons of humility. Just as a diamond is transformed from a piece of coal, spiritual living is the same. It is a simple matter of time and pressure. Our changes occur in God's time and not our own as we have many experiences to witness before they become part of us. The pressure comes from weariness of feeling bad and trying to become better individuals and people. The more we put into our dependence on God and personal development, the greater the changes will become. It all happens at the precise right time. Time and pressure are great allies.

The Bible is the complete story of man and his quest for better living and understanding. There are many wonderful stories of personal struggles to establish deeper connectivity with our Creator and understanding of our purpose in the universe. When Jesus walked this earth and became our Teacher and Savior, people thirsted for His words and direction and followed Him. If you have never read it or, have trouble understanding the Bible, I highly recommend reading "The Sermon On The Mount" by the late Emmett Fox. It is a fascinating and vital book! I have given away many copies of this book over the years and I have read it hundreds of times as well as his other works. When I read this particular book, it opened up a completely new dimension for me and I came to understand the Bible much better. Christ taught the absolute truth of man and his relationship to The Father, how we should live together and the peace and harmony we could attain for the asking. He taught divine love, and care and treatment for our ills by way of humility. In every facet of the human experience, we are gifted with spirituality. This is how we fill those empty voids. We humbly ask God to remove our flaws and accept us exactly as we are. There was a nice woman who asked me this morning how does she know when she has humility? I explained to her that her own question answers itself. Any time we are asking how, what, when, or where in the spirit of growth, we are practicing humility. We are confessing we do not know and wish to learn. Our development is a never-ending process with unlimited possibilities because it is our *daily bread*. It is the food and water from our Father that sustains us spiritually, emotionally, and mentally. This is of course dependent upon our daily maintenance.

As humans, we are spirits trapped inside our physical bodies for the duration of time on earth. We thirst for more of that which makes us better. We are mere vessels. If we walk down to the riverbank with a pint vessel, we can only carry back a pint. If we take a quart, we can bring back a quart. If we set our camp upon the bank itself, (our relationship with God), we can drink anytime we wish. The possibilities of our spiritual experience are precisely the same. This is true of all creatures God has created and of creation itself. Spirits are all around us all the time. We need only to acknowledge them and allow them to be free. We find we are a part of endless supply and demand. We will certainly be given that which we really need and our life itself demands that we give back unto it. I think it very neat it works this way.

Humility is often a difficult subject of discussion but it need not be that way. The moment we claim we have it, it is out the window. When I searched for it, I was chasing the elusive. I found that by doing the next right thing to nurture others and myself, humility would find me. Is it not actually the answer from God to all our prayers? It is not a possession rather it is a loaned gift. I think of it as an angel lighting upon my shoulders for a moment. We have a goldfish pond in our backyard with an arbor and park-bench that I constructed on a Mothers' Day weekend for my wife while she was away. It is a very tranquil place where she enjoys sitting and reading. A few years ago I was sitting out there one fine day playing my guitar and a hummingbird landed on one of the tuners of the guitar for a very few seconds. This overwhelming feeling of connectivity shot through me, then it was gone. Sometimes a fleeting glimpse can be all we need to know at the time and so it is with humility. We may see it, feel it, share it, but it is not to be captured. My Creator sends me these special trinkets often and it makes me wonder about those I may have missed due to lack of awareness or being in self-will. If I compare the struggles I have known to the special gifts I have received, life is definitely worthwhile and should be lived to the fullest. Let us count our blessings and even write our special moments down on paper to help us remember should we have a dark day and forget.

In your waking hour each day, when your mind is clean and clear, allow yourself to be still with your Father and your thoughts, and then *talk* to Him. You never have to look for God because He is never lost. We are the ones that get lost or out of touch at times. It will *always* bring about positive results with each day, filled with new demonstrations and experiences. Life is beautiful; get out in the middle of the carnival! Let your soul soar as if it were a helium-filled balloon.

13 | Unity and Service

We can do together what none of us can do alone! Is this anything other than the extension of un-conditional love and compassion? The most spiritual thing I ever do is ask for help and guidance. I know very little on my own, and without the support of others, I would surely fade into noth- ingness. This is the time in our life that we become the river itself instead of just the finely polished rocks which cover its bed. We are in a constant cycle that we consume and distribute. We become a part of a spiritual circle, which for all practical reason is impregnable. We find ourselves in amazingly profound relationships we had never dreamed. Within this circle, other circles are born that swell out like a stone thrown into a still pond, spreading to magnificence. This is what I know as the presence of God. As humans, we are only a very small particle of wholeness. Though man may never become pure, his spirit may be quite capable. I have had the great honor of knowing such people. We can experience purity any time we turn to God and Jesus and be with them any time we so desire. Life is not about perfec- tion it is about making progress from a diseased condition.

Again I will say, "God does not want you holy, He wants you healed".

I am convinced that several gifts in my personal life were born by the grace of God. First is my relationship with my Creator, then my life in this fellowship of Alcoholics Anonymous, my family of blood, and my brothers and sisters in fellowship. This wonderful program has millions of members whose lives have completely transformed. We practice sponsorship, (spiritual mentors), supporting one another with unconditional love, patience, and tolerance. Those we take under wing, we call pigeons. My sponsor (Bill Roop) is a very wise and spiritually fit man who is ninety years young. He has been sober for fifty-five years and for him I have the deepest affection, respect and admiration. He is so much like my grandfather who was the most spiritual person I have ever known. My life does not include many problems or drama these days but what I know about this great man is that we can have a wonderful conver-sation without speaking a word. If I went to him with a prob-lem, I already know what his answer would be. He would ask me if I have prayed about it and as I would reply yes, he would then ask why I am bothering him about it. He has tre-mendously helped me with connectivity that I pass along to those I take under wing and work with. To me, this sums up unity, service, and recovery (the three legacies of A.A.). I had recently asked him to perform my own eulogy when the time comes and he asked me "did I not have a minister?" He is a great *administer* in my mind and heart and I could not imag-ine anyone more qualified and perfect for the duty.

Unity in this world begins the day we cease to fight it and align ourselves with it. I have heard the statement "I hope I can be half the man my dog thinks I am". I hope I can depart with a quarter of the love, compassion, and trust Toby has for me. He is a little male Yorkie that weighs about five pounds. He has a hundred pound heart. Toby and I are very united. Just around two years of age now, he has been a God- given gift. Since I have had him as a puppy, he sleeps against my chest and puts all four paws in my hand in a fetal position. I ask him each night if he is ready to go to bed and he runs ahead of me, jumps up on the bed bouncing up and down, and with his front paws he pulls back our bed covers. I can play my acoustic guitar and he sits and listens. When I plug in an electric guitar and turn the volume down low, he starts singing his little heart out. We have traveled many miles together and we are inseparable. He is not mine in a possessive sense; rather he is a wonderful soul whom I am gratefully gifted. We share a fabulous bond equal to the greatest loves in my life. Not one single time has he ever betrayed me. I stand in awe of the connections we experience upon this plane. They are so simple and contain such clarity, man often forgets to give praise and acknowledge his wonderful gifts.

It is obvious God's intention for man's soul is to be filled with love and compassion, and destined to survive. What would we be and where would we be without it? Unity is the strongest human foundation of principles I know that we can share together on an equal scale. What do we want from life? What do we seek? What are our visions of the future other than today's dreams? The answers have been in place since the beginning of time. We have, in many cases become blinded by the material world from the actual truths of our purpose. In life, we can easily get into severe trouble, but these are the clutches we wish to grow beyond. When we cease fighting others, we become a part of serenity and live in a solution rather than the problem. We settle down to the important matters of life that are the essence of simplicity. Unity, service, and recovery, and are the most treasured and valuable prospects known to the human race. There is safety and strength in numbers. When we unite and care for each other, personal and collective recovery will shortly follow. We become a part of the whole. A miracle that is divinely inspired spreads among us. As our unity grows, so does our ability to help others along the way in love and compassion. We quickly learn the importance of service to others.

Serving others is the complete summation of the Christ. It is what He did. The demonstration of washing the feet of His disciples was monumental. The definition of monumental is; serving as a monument and enduring. It was also a strong message of equality. Romans 1 verse 11 states "For I long to see you, that I may impart unto you some spiritual gift, to the end ye may be established". This is not a mere vision; it is reality that works perfectly and under any condition. Come as you are. It is also the ultimate antidote for ego inflation. We may very well come across some that it seems we cannot help in any other way but to pray for them. Prayer is action and we take it. The results always remain in God's hands. There were people who tried to help me years before I became completely defeated. Sometimes it seems that they were about to help me to death. Today, I fully believe it was their prayers that set everything in motion so that I would come to surrender. My life is no longer about me. It is about *us*. In unity and service, we become *established*. Life is not about outcomes but rather the efforts we make. It is not about quantity of relationships it is about the quality. This beautiful chapter in the book of Romans gives us a perfect diagram of unity, service, and recovery from the eyes and soul of Paul who came to follow the gospel of God.

God and Son wish to meet you and give unto you spiritual gifts just as you are. The question remains, have you met yourself?

Have you decided to separate from self-will and presently seek Gods will? The above passage clearly states that He will be with us through all our efforts to make the transition or our path toward it. A furry little caterpillar with many legs crawls upon the ground, and in a tree it spins itself into a dark cocoon and later reappears as a beautiful butterfly. That which once crawled upon the ground now flies. Nature often tells us all we need to know about ourselves. Metamorphosis also happens in the human experience. The old dies away and beauty is born. We have transitioned back from self-will (our design) unto free will (God's design). What is important is that we make the trip successfully! YEA!!! Our transition is pragmatic, leaving nothing in question. Either we make this step or we remain in darkness, exactly like being in a cocoon. The human transition usually takes much longer to evolve. In fact, it takes the remainder of our life. As long as we are breathing, our journey is not completed, but what a beautiful journey it really is. Mine begins anew every day because I never have any idea what God will put in front of me to absorb.

I am inclined to believe that service to others is the greatest gift entrusted to us from the hand of our Creator. Sharing with others what we have found is a great responsibility. Far removed from self-righteousness, as we extend love, compassion and understanding, we may never know it but we may be actually saving the life of another. The outcome is none of our business. What is important is that we pass along a message of hope, unity, and equality. I am so grateful these selfless people were here when I arrived. Otherwise, I feel certain I would have died. They gave of themselves generously and I came to see a spark of hope succeeded by a vision of becoming a part of a wondrous society. Ever so slowly and usually painfully, I began to grow out of the darkness of whom and what I was, into the light of what I could be if willing to do some work. Had these others not been there I would have had no idea of the task ahead and I certainly could not have understood how to approach it with the little intellect I had. A large part of my happiness today hinges on the fact that the longer I am around, the more I realize how little I actually know. God's love and care is never ending and all fulfilling.

We make great sacrifices for the good of the whole. For that, we only become stronger individually and collectively. What is it that separates humankind but the diseases of self? If you do not believe the seven deadly sins are alive and well, watch the world news on any given day. The only way to overcome evil is to overcome with good and it begins inside each individual. Leave the evil in the hands of He who has power to correct it. When will man transform from soldiers of destruction into soldiers of instruction? I like to think it is catching on, and man one day will rise above to become soldiers of real fortune. The wrath of God is exactly what it says it is, so why does man continue to play God in a role He would have absolutely no part? I fail to understand the complexities and insanity when there is such a simple solution as the practice of unity, service, and recovery. However, that is just me! I should also acknowledge that I am not the brightest star in the sky. It is perfectly normal to cry out "I do not know and I do not understand". This is exactly why we are here together, to help each other through the difficulties in life. We serve one another with love and compassion, which becomes the reason for existence. Allow your life to move in passion for it is from that deep place in your heart it cries out.

My earlier years in A.A. were deeply involved with service work, which was an honor to do. I served on a few committees and dedicated five years of volunteering in prisons and in various other ways. In the spirit of rotation, I stepped down to give the opportunities to others. I am still involved in service but mostly I sit on the sideline and give others a chance. It keeps me centered in the fact that I have no desire to run any show. I remain pleased watching others as their faces light up from being a part of a wonderful society. They are mending, healing, and improving their own quality of life, and a message of hope continues to flow perfectly in a divine order. My physical disability affects some of my involvement today and sometimes I am doing good to show up, maybe lead a discussion, or work with another individual. Sometimes I may help someone with a few dollars. The greatest thing I believe I accomplish is to take another to the message instead of thinking I am a messenger. I give rides to meetings, make coffee, and refer people to literature, passages from the Bible, and so-forth. I am perfectly content being a channel, in which God works through me. I am no more or no less. I am just a child on a spiritual playground.

Magic occurs when we extend love and care to others. At any given time, we may come across someone who has a heavy heart for one reason or another. I have found that my real ambition has long been to comfort and help in any reasonable way I may be capable. My capacity is in direct proportion to my willingness to do God's bidding. My desire is to live a useful life for my remaining time, and it has been so for a long time. It brings strength to others and me as well. My needs are fulfilled and my wants are very few. The ability in us all to bring someone from tears to laughter is a very gratifying experience. It is not about what we have done but rather what God has done through us. We all have this ability provided our own house is in order. We cannot give away what we do not have yet we can pray for guidance. People have asked me questions before and I would have to ask them to give me a few minutes to think about their question. I do not have their answers but God does. A great deal of the time they have their own answers and simply do not realize it. "Pray about it" is the best response I share with anyone. Sure, I may share experience and hope but they are on their journey and I have no right to interfere.

We are all going to experience some very emotional times in our lives. Running away, denying or blocking it out by some other means is not a solution. Instead, be with it and care for it. If employed, we are allotted sick days and most of the time this is the very best thing we can do. Grab a box of tissue, crawl into bed and be sick. Cry from the depths of your heart if need be. This is not weakness; it is the process of healing. My greatest strengths derived from my lowest points. You will get to the other side of your situation. Some matters may take a very long time such as the loss of a loved one. How do we handle such times? We do not! We turn it over to God and go through the grieving process. We acknowledge love never ends, nor should we ever attempt to cease what is in our hearts. We experience the inner change and serenity waits beyond the storm. Each night I thank God for what I have, what He has taken away, and what is left. Such a simple and short prayer that I have found to be most useful in the darkest of times. We are united and we have served others. Now comes a time to cry out, I need help! This is recovery in motion. There is no beginning or end to this circle of completion.

My unity and service is first and foremost to God. Everything else that occurs is in His time and not mine. He has created the entire universe, including that which is light years away, so how could I be so arrogant to say He is in my time. God does not exist in time though He is with us, loves and cares for us, and knows all. He is not of our time even though He walks with us. Time is a measure and He cannot be measured nor calculated. In the short life of Jesus, He knew this and taught The Father was forevermore. Here again we see the ripple effect that the teachings of Jesus would swell out as the ripples upon a pond and remain timeless. I think it is extremely amazing and powerful that we as individuals are a part. It is not important to me how long I have been here, how long I may remain, what I have done or should have done. What is important is that I have been a small particle of the great experience.

As we continue upon our path, it is important to stop at times and witness where we are, what has evolved and where we wish to go. The very next person who comes onto our path can change everything, as we have to search deeper and more meaningful. Those we extend to, change us probably more than we can dream of changing them, which is an area we need, not visit. How life is working for you and what I can do to help are the only two true questions I ever ask. God never asks any more of a person, so how could we? We can only rest in reason and move in passion.

14 | Changing Course

Are you a newcomer to a twelve-step program or spiritual living, otherwise? We all are. No matter how long we have searched each day is new and full of more experiences. Your time here in human experience is especially for you. Psalm 110 verse 3 states:"Thy people shall be willing in the day of thy power, in the beauties of holiness from the womb of the morning: thou hast the dew of thy youth." This incredible passage clearly explains that we are only granted a single day, but with it comes the new, the fresh, and the undiscovered. The most important word in the passage is willing or willingness. Changes will not arrive without willingness. It is impossible. This also states firmly that in our waking hour we should be devotional no matter what our daily schedule may consist. Every awakening is a day of power should we choose to live in it The beauty given each day, through God and Jesus Christ, allows each of us to live in a more positive manner. If you can come to terms with and fully understand the power of this short passage, there remains nothing to worry about, nothing to fear and no underlying motives or designs. The question that remains is; are we now willing to surrender all we have known? How it is and how it could be is what I focus upon, as it allows the opportunity to adjust perception. The dew of thy youth translates to the current moment in our life. It does not say that such a time may come or that we may acquire it, it states it is gifted for us to utilize now.

The years of believing the measure of a man was how much he could take and remain upright on his feet, were not wasted years at all. To the contrary, it was a time of evolving towards the surrender of self-will. It is only in surrender that we plug into power. It was the beginning of an end, that new beginnings became possible. As children of God we are fragile and vulnerable, and this is rightly so as we walk into the light of dependence upon our Creator. This is not just theory it is proof of life. It works very well should we choose it and it is a matter of making the simple choice. Who among us would choose to have their soul bound to gravity as our feet, when the soul can rise above gravitational force and soar like an eagle? Humans are creatures of habit and in many cases meet change with resistance. We tend to stay in a comfort zone of what we currently think instead of stepping outside the box and into the unknown. I lived in the same manner for many years, doing the same things expecting different results. Eventually the pressure became unbearable. It was apparent the time had come to *change my course* and take a chance with the unknown. In reality I had not made a choice, rather I was driven there by the existence of chaos that shot through every thread of my mind and body. It was after the dust had settled that I began making different choices. There first had to be willingness to get outside the box.

Man invests great sums of money for paintings by the famous artists of our time. Authors write wonderful books and musicians create beautiful music that can take the human mind many places and do very well financially. I love them all for their talents and dedication and inner souls. The greatest artist of any kind is you. You are your greatest investment as you walk with God. You are His child, a masterpiece that may be similar to others, but there is no duplicate of yourself. Our dividends arrive when we give away all we know to be good and truthful to others. All that for which we have strived, we give away freely. I do not consider myself a great writer nor do I desire money for any of my work. I make investments in people, **Period!** I possess the greatest wealth I can fathom, and I am definitely not alone.

I have never been alone. Even in the years that the concept of God seemed so far away, He was with me all along, patiently waiting for me to become ready and willing. I am not telling you that walking a spiritual path will always be easy. In fact, there will be many difficulties to overcome upon your journey. What I *can* tell you is that just when you think life cannot get any better, it does.

Perhaps in time the human race will experience its own resurrection. Humans are not completely naive. We turn on the news and see citizens attempting to overthrow their governing systems. Wars are being fought and the needless slaughter of God's children is an undeniable fact. People are hungry and live in poverty and the hunger is not just for food. These matters all derive from the seven deadly sins, which are; pride, greed, envy, lust, sloth, anger, and gluttony. My opinion is that they are running rampant. Each of these sins is created by humans, yet they are not fit for human consumption. It is at this point I have to find a separate reality, or else return to insanity. If these matters are, in essence, reality, then reality is a lie. If told this is reality and we must accept it, that too is a lie. Reconsider for a moment that Jesus had only one test for any situation; does it work? I think we can all agree it is not working very well at all. Perhaps the time is growing nearer that we will set aside the divisions of the countries and the ways that are clearly not working. Maybe we could become united citizens of the world. It is easy to say no, this cannot happen, but can humankind continue to exist as we currently are? People have a habit of thinking if they discuss their deeper thoughts and feelings someone is going to label them as a *whack job.* In this instance, are we not placing other people's opinions ahead of God? I may be a whack job myself but I invite you to come along for a while and then reevaluate your position. You can always return to your reality as previously dictated to you. There is nothing to lose in this simple proposition.

Our future does not rest in the radical and fanatical. It has to grow more toward neutrality. We must look with better eyes and deeper hearts if we wish to resort to sane living. If you read the St. Francis prayer you will find that its contents are a complete diagram for spiritual living in the realm of sobriety, which is sane, rational thinking and actions. Humans suffer many addictions that continue intoxicating life. It is my prayer that this chain of intoxication be broken sooner rather than later, that we may all get on with the luxury of living peacefully and respectfully. There is only one ultimate authority and that is God, whatever you wish to call Him, and I pray that you find Him/Her. It is there that the healing process, individually and collectively, will begin and continue as long as pursued.

"Changing Course" is not a theory. It is an action. I know this because it has been my *true experience* upon this earth and I know from my own spiritual wealth that you will experience your life more fully as you walk your path and regain your identity. Claim your identity with God. If there is anything you take from this that has been helpful, please pass it on. If so, my purpose in this life of unity and service fulfills me and you will be fulfilling the lives of others.

God Bless You

Gary Watson

CPSIA information can be obtained at www.ICGtesting.com
Printed in the USA
LVOW112317230512

283036LV00001B/46/P